A FORCE OF ONES

A
FORCE
OF
ONES

Reclaiming Individual Power
in a Time of Teams, Work Groups,
and Other Crowds

Stanley M. Herman

Jossey-Bass Publishers • San Francisco

Substantial discounts on bulk quantities of Jossey-Bass books are available to corporations, professional associations, and other organizations. For details and discount information, contact the special sales department at Jossey-Bass Inc., Publishers. (415) 433-1740; Fax (415) 433-0499.

For sales outside the United States, contact Maxwell Macmillan International Publishing Group, 866 Third Avenue, New York, New York 10022.

Manufactured in the United States of America

The paper used in this book is acid-free and meets the State of California requirements for recycled paper (50 percent recycled waste, including 10 percent postconsumer waste), which are the strictest guidelines for recycled paper currently in use in the United States.

10% POST CONSUMER WASTE

The dust jacket is printed on stock that contains 80 percent postconsumer waste and is chlorine free.

80% POST CONSUMER WASTE

Library of Congress Cataloging-in-Publication Data

Herman, Stanley M., date.
    A force of ones : reclaiming individual power in a time of teams, work groups, and other crowds / Stanley M. Herman.
       p. cm. — (Jossey-Bass management series)
    Includes bibliographical references and index.
    ISBN 1-55542-561-5
    1. Work groups. 2. Interpersonal relations. 3. Individuality.
I. Title. II. Series.
HD66.H47   1994
650.1′3—dc20
                                     93-23617
                                        CIP

FIRST EDITION
HB Printing   10 9 8 7 6 5 4 3 2 1   *Code 9401*

To Georgia Herman,
who read each one of these pages
three times or more and helped to keep me on track,
or at least from going off track too badly

Contents

CONTENTS

Exercises

Preface

You and I live and work in an era of global markets, worldwide corporate alliances, and mega programs, and the intricate interdependent organizational relationships that are essential to these human undertakings. The age of the single craftsman or craftswoman producing a personal creation is all but gone. Now almost all work has become so complex and segmented that it requires collections of people to perform. Most management and organizational experts in the last decade have been focusing their study and the advice they give to operating managers on how to stimulate the involvement of such collections of people and draw upon their combined knowledge, a process that in current organizational terminology is called group empowerment.

A *Force of Ones* is a manual for individual survival in these big-system, group-oriented times. I don't argue against the reality of today's organizational interdependencies, but I do say that focusing almost exclusively on groups, teams, and other collectives is creating an imbalance and becoming counterproductive. Groups and teams are useful and satisfying for some purposes, but they can be frustrating and worse than useless for others.

A Force of Ones focuses on what you and I as single individuals can be and can do at work. Managers cannot really empower groups to be inventive or courageous, to confront tough issues rather than avoid them, or to choose courses of action that are unfamiliar and uncomfortable to individual group members. Only individuals can see beyond conventionally popular views, depart from consensus and stand for an unpopular position, generate a personal, driving vision that will inspire others to take a new direction, or risk resources and personal reputation to achieve a vision. And managers cannot compel individuals to be empowered; individuals have to empower themselves.

Audience

I address this book to managers, those who aspire to manage, and all those employees who want to know what they can do to make a place for themselves in their organizations—to do more than just fill a slot—where they will be called on to make creative and productive contributions and from which in return they can derive both success and personal satisfaction.

Whatever your position, my goal is to encourage and guide you in identifying your own particular strengths, honing them, and using them to get what you want out of your life and organizational career. My goal is also to show that individuality is important to organizations as well as to persons and that if you don't recognize the individual characteristics of an organization (whether a small work group or a giant corporation), you are doomed to prescribe and follow mass remedies (such as team-building, zero-based budgeting, or TQM) that often treat the wrong problem.

I want *A Force of Ones* to be a book that earns itself a long-term lease on your bookshelf, a book that you pull down from time to time as your career progresses. The subjects and tools it covers apply to specialists and people in other nonmanagerial jobs as well as at all levels of management. Whatever your position, you will find ideas worth understanding about people who occupy other levels: what their worlds look like to them, how they can lose their focus, and how by getting back to the basics of their individuality, they can find their focus again. You may be surprised to learn the thinking that lies behind some of the apparently irrational acts of your boss or subordinate.

Overview of the Contents

The Introduction explores what it means to reclaim your individualism and use it. The remainder of the book is divided into four major parts, each based on a theme.

Part One, "Tapping into Your Singular Vision," describes how we individually build many of the most formidable barriers to doing what we want to do and satisfying ourselves. Often, these self-imposed prohibitions don't serve the "culturally correct" purposes we think they will. The chapters in Part One suggest a number of options for discovering and refining what you, as an individual, want to do and for making your input and influence felt in basic one-on-one (*mano-a-mano*) interactions with others in your organization. I also speak directly to managers about the reality (in contrast to the mythology) of management work. Despite the conventional view of management as a planning and control function, management is mainly a job of reacting to unforeseen demands. Part One provides tools for cutting through time-consuming rituals, identifying what is important and what is not, and tapping into your own and other people's energy and skills to make things happen.

Part Two, "Staying Centered in Key Work Relationships," shows you how to recognize and tailor your own version of the skills you need to improve your power and personal satisfaction, in other words, to get better at what you do and enjoy it more. Prerequisites for this process are taking time to step off the treadmill of your regular routines to check out what is working for you and what isn't, then making a *small* number of adjustments that are practical for you as an individual person. Part Two focuses especially on working relationships with bosses and subordinates. It identifies ways of obtaining relatively honest impressions of how your boss and your employees see you, and ways to tell the difference between what is important in that information and what is just static.

Part Three, "Organizations Are Individuals, Too," deals with individualism as an underlying orientation and operative value of groups ranging in size from small project teams to whole companies. Organizations vary critically in their character and stage of development, and what is right for one can be dead wrong for another. No organization can improve on all dimensions at the same time—there simply are not enough time, resources, and energy. Whether you are a specialist, a supervisor, or a CEO, you have to make choices. Those choices will be good ones only if they fit with the individual character and situation of your organization. Otherwise, though they may conform to the latest popular improvement program, they'll waste time, money, and worst of all, the investment of people's spirit.

In Part Three, I explore the advantages and disadvantages of participative management and employee involvement and suggest when participative approaches are likely to be useful and when they are likelier to be self-defeating. It is important to distinguish between at least two kinds of team formation: the general inclusion group (GIG) for working on gradual, incremental improvement in productivity, and the individual initiative network (IIN) for developing major discontinuous changes in response to high-challenge problems or opportunities.

I also talk about conflict in organizations and some of the options for dealing with it when both parties are genuinely willing to resolve their issues, as opposed to times when the other guy is really out to get you. And I look at major programs to change organizational cultures, focusing on why total quality management, organization excellence, or any of a long line of similar pop programs with catchy slogans often produce such limited results. Unless the right *individuals* (starting at the top) concentrate on a *few* carefully selected objectives, both time and dollar resources will probably be dissipated, with few results to show for it. Given today's high level of investment in major organizational improvement programs, it is important that what is likely to be useful and what is not be generally understood, by individuals at all levels rather than just by specialist administrators and top executives. Only then can the ideas and activities of big-system proposals be tested for realism by the people who are supposed to make them work.

Part Four, "Customs of Command and Arts of the Possible," concludes *A Force of Ones*. It encourages readers to recognize that *power* and *politics* are not necessarily dirty words. Instead, they are inescapable elements in human interactions. Here, I ask you if you do or don't want to be a serious player in organizational power and politics, and I suggest some ways you can control your choices. Whether or not you choose to play in this series of games, it's important for you to understand them, at least at a rudimentary level; so a set of political tactics (of the softball variety) is presented for your practical use. The book closes with a commentary on the spirit of individualism and a recap of the basics for finding and expressing more of your own individualism.

At the end of each chapter, I have included a page of notes containing points particularly worth remembering. There is also space for you to add your own notes. The book also contains many exercises and guidelines. They are designed to be understood and used quickly on the job. All were originally developed for practical use in organizations, including very large corporations, small businesses, government agencies, and even volunteer church and charity groups. In addition, *A Force of Ones* features stories and poems. Stories lend depth and human subtlety to intellectual points and prescriptions, and poems allow a writer to say more in fewer words and, it is hoped, a reader to hear more.

Acknowledgments

I would like to thank the people who contributed (over three decades) to this book's existence and content. Many at the

Gestalt Institute of Cleveland helped me to see things in new ways. A veritable corps of organizational and management consultants at General Electric Company and TRW taught me practical skills and tactics. I especially want to thank the clients I worked with in ways that helped both them and me discover what was useful (and what was not). And a special thanks, too, to Steven Katten, my "sanity checker"; Sarah Polster, whose determination made this a better book than it would otherwise have been; and Geoffrey Bellman, who in some mysterious way helped me start the project.

Escondido, California   Stanley M. Herman
December 1993

The Author

STANLEY M. HERMAN consults to senior and middle managers both in major corporations and in smaller public and private organizations on organizational effectiveness. For more than a decade, he has studied the management styles and career progress of a group of managers and executives in several industries, focusing particularly on the critical factors in their individual advancement (and, sometimes, decline).

Herman is the author of *The People Specialists* (1968) and, with Michael Korenich, *Authentic Management* (1977), which was translated into Japanese. He has also written scores of articles for management publications, and columns for newspapers and magazines, and has appeared in management films and videos. He is the principal developer of Authentic Management, a pioneering approach to contingency management, and he has taught at several universities, including the University of Southern California; the University of California, Los Angeles; the University of Richmond; the University of Wisconsin; Pepperdine University's Master of Science in Organization Development program; the Federal Executive Institute; as well as in other professional development programs.

A FORCE OF ONES

Reclaiming the Power of the Individual

A *Force of Ones* addresses people working in organizations. It asserts that the thoughts, decisions, and actions of individuals—single, solitary persons—are critically important, both to the individuals themselves and to their organizations, a fact that has tended to get lost in the attention most organizational authorities have given to work groups and large organizational units over the last decade. The simplest way to express the point is this: *all human organizations, no matter how simple or complex, large or small, are based on interaction between individuals. Therefore, a crucial element of the success or failure of an enterprise depends on the results of interaction between key individuals.*

If the CEO can't find a way to convince a key board member, there will be no acquisition this year. If the product design manager doesn't come back to her boss time after time to argue for the introduction of new technology rather than a face-lift for the old product, the company may fall behind its competition irreparably. If the employee who works in the clean room doesn't believe what the company trainer is saying about quality or thinks it's against his best interests, he won't change his way of operating. And he will communicate his viewpoint to his fellow workers.

For the individual, the organization is one of life's arenas, a place where friends and opponents are made, "sports" are played, and contests held—for fun and profit by some, for human betterment or a strongly held principle by others, and for a personal sense of victory or accomplishment by still others. These diverse motives are part of the yeasty whole of organizations, and they give balance and energy to each other. As a player, the individual in this arena has the opportunity to exercise his or her abilities, to discover new knowledge and old wisdom. He or she will encounter joys that elate and disappointments that temper. He or she can experience the strength that derives from marching in solid phalanx with the collective view, and that other strength that can only be found when the individual stands alone, apart from the collective view.

A *Force of Ones* is for people who work in organizations. It is for both managers and nonmanagers who recognize managing as more art than science and who want to know how to apply their own and others' individuality in ways that produce more relevant and inventive solutions to problems and increase work satisfaction and pleasure. It is for people who have grown skeptical about management preachments that are offered as cure-alls for what ails everybody.

This book about reclaiming your individual power and using it effectively in your organization is based on two assumptions: that there are not a few but *many* routes to a successful and satisfying career and that your unique character, inclinations, and talents can be put to good use in addressing the issues and opportunities that you confront in your work and life and through which you achieve success and satisfaction.

Individualism Today

Individualism is an old-fashioned word that hasn't been popular for a while. It's also a word for which no easy, up-to-date euphemism can be found—though I tried. *Self-empowerment* comes close but doesn't quite capture the spirit of independence that individualism carries with it.

At the time of the founding of our country, in the perspective of Thomas Jefferson, Alexander Hamilton, Thomas Paine, Benjamin Franklin, and indeed most of our early leaders, the importance of the individual and his or her rights to "life, liberty and the pursuit of happiness" were crucial. Through the nineteenth century and into the middle of the twentieth, individuality and its accompanying traditions of independence, self-reliance, and personal initiative were admired, especially in the Westward movement of the pioneers and later in the rags-to-riches tales of our early entrepreneurs. Devotion to individual rights and opportunities was viewed throughout most of the world as the core of American ideals.

In the gradual transition to urbanization and industrialization, however, exploitation of working people and excesses among the very wealthy and powerful became more prevalent in American culture, and somehow the word *individualism* came to be associated with these deeds. Later, in the mid seventies, there was a renewed downgrading of individualism, perhaps in reaction to the hippie culture of the previous decade and what seemed to be its excessive emphasis on "dropping out" of mainstream society in favor of self-gratification, perhaps in recognition of the increasingly complex and difficult issues that seemed to pit community requirements against individual rights.

For whatever reasons, individualism has become a "politically incorrect" notion in this era. Many think that the world's people and activities are too interdependent and globally interlinked for individualism. Others automatically equate individualism with ruthlessness, authoritarianism, and greed. They see the large-scale corruption and financial manipulations of the go-go eighties as the awful results of unchecked individualism.

Reclaiming Your Individualism

But individualism is not defined by selfishness, ruthlessness, or greed. An individual may act either selfishly or generously, ruthlessly or considerately. Instead, individualism is primarily defined by independence of thought, feeling, and action. It is, in other words, based on recognizing and appreciating one's own internal signals. That means:

• *You get your authoritative answers from yourself.* You may listen to experts, bosses, a group you belong to, or those in power, but your ultimate check is made against your own standards. The final seal of approval is yours alone. That may be a scary prospect, especially if you think of yourself as often unsure of your position. (Finding your own particular core of confidence is one of the subjects of this book.)

• *You tune in to your own personal vision for your life and career.*

4

You don't make up that vision from fashionable pieces of the latest pop culture models. You discover it, work with it, develop it, and change it as you go along. It's yours.

- *You use yourself as your own best instrument in making your vision work.* You sharpen (or tune) your awareness of what is important in your environment and your confidence and power for dealing with what you identify. Gradually, you tap into your sources of knowledge and capability, which have been covered over with cumulative layers of self-doubt. As you take these steps, the instrument that is you gets better and better at doing what you want it to do.

- *You become more powerful.* This happens not because someone else lays more authority on you, or because you become part of a clique or power group. Instead, you personally, all by yourself, become internally stronger and surer of yourself and your ideas. Your new power is quickly recognized by people with whom you interact. When you are powerful, you can work with individuals, groups, or whole establishments from a position of strength. And when necessary, you can work without them, or even against them, and sometimes get your way.

- *You become both more exhilarated and more calm.* And sometimes both at the same time. You are more exhilarated because when you are clear about what *you* want it becomes your personal target not just the group's goal. You are calmer because you have fewer of those gnawing nervous doubts about how things will turn out.

- *You become more honest because there are fewer reasons to lie.* In June of 1992, a president of Russia addressed the U.S. congress for the first time in history. His loudest standing ovation came when he promised "No more lies." Of course, that statement is likely to turn out to be an exaggeration, but it represents a direction that Americans seem to want, and not just from a foreign statesman. That same year, a third-party presidential candidate became a phenomenon in U.S. politics, drawing strong support from all parts of the political spectrum. His appeal clearly wasn't based on his positions on issues (which were largely unannounced), but on his personal straightforwardness. Whether in the form of politicians telling constituents what they want to hear, top executives giving lip service to environmental cleanup commitments, or ordinary citizens promising "I'll call you back," or "the check's in the mail," the art of lying has been developed into a fine art over recent years. Most of us complain about it but do not do much else. "After all," we say, "everybody does it." But individuals with internal strength lie a lot less. It's not a matter of morality, but a matter of practicality. Truth works better for them. It comes out of their mouths more naturally and carries more impact.

• *You become stronger as well as more powerful.* There's a paradox that often appears. The more personally powerful you get, the more clearly you are able to see and hear other people. When your own point of view is unclouded and held with steady confidence, no one can change it except yourself. Abruptly, you become free. Free to see and hear and understand your opposition, even to appreciate their perspectives. When you are strong, it's easier to be generous. Not with the trifling generosity that comes from meeting your expected obligations, but with a full-hearted kindness that simply and naturally moves you to actions.

6

Individualism alone automatically produces neither a positive nor negative impact on society as a whole. The impact that an individual has is a product of aspects of his or her personality and character that individualism releases for action.

Individualism and Big Systems

The point is often made that the world has grown too complex and interdependent for individualism. But it is just this complexity and global linkage that *require* individualism if they are not to produce merely a renovated, technology-enhanced version of insensitive bureaucracy. Connecting a series of poorly manufactured metal links, no matter in what length or pattern, does not produce a reliable chain. Joining together a series of risk-avoidant, habit-addicted, turf-protecting functionaries is not likely to produce a team or network well prepared to integrate its efforts and meet the challenges of rapidly changing technologies or markets. The joined efforts of venturesome people ready to initiate and risk, willing to identify and straightforwardly negotiate differences, and able to inspire others' support through their individual credibility, are much more likely to accomplish their goals.

Group-imposed imperatives about manners, methods, and models can be oppressive. For organizations in need of radical change in order to prepare for the future, or even survive, group imperatives are almost invariably restrictive. An organization may get moderate improvements from teams that fixate on including everybody's contribution, but it probably won't get step-function breakthroughs or new directions. In remarks to the press, James Baker, secretary of state in the Bush administration, once said that negotiations in large international groups were often necessary and usually long and agonizingly painful. He contrasted this to the rapid, creative, and successful solution to an international trade problem that came about from the efforts of a small State Department team, single-mindedly dedicated to causing a satisfactory change. The principle of individualism can encourage the gathering together of clear-minded, collaborative but separate persons into a powerful network for accomplishing substantial purposes.

My Personal Orientation

As far back as I can remember I've been captivated by the questions, "What's it all about? and, How does it work?" I've asked those basic questions of others, myself, and as a management consultant, my clients. Getting back to these basics has frequently produced new and potentially important perspectives. What I've learned over time, however, is that when the answers to the questions are based solely on logically derived, reasoned responses those answers have only limited use.

Many people, especially those in the behavioral sciences, have long recognized that "facts" alone are not sufficient for understanding what occurs in human processes. Emotions, belief systems, biases, and feelings of all sorts can influence and even distort the ways people see and deal with facts. I personally did not come to this realization until I was past thirty, fairly late in comparison to most, I suppose, but I had grown up in an age that revered logic, science, and cause and effect rationality.

My first experience in how influential the "soft," unmeasurable factors were came dramatically when I attended (under some duress) my first sensitivity-training session, sponsored by the Fortune 100 company I then worked for. I mostly watched as others in the group—conventional, competent midlevel managers—interacted with each other in ways I had never seen before, ways that sometimes revealed resentment, envy, anger, affection, and empathy. I realized abruptly that these emotions were not just products of the training-session situations. They were present all the time, even in the day-to-day workplace, except there they were mostly kept hidden and emerged only indirectly.

Being who I was and how I was at that time, my initial reaction to these soft factors was to think of them as additional data to add to the management equation. I was taught a new management model: it was right to be nonjudgmental and to be a good listener. It was wrong to be defensive and authoritarian. Those in authority should facilitate the participation of their subordinates in decision making, rather than make decisions themselves. I learned, too, that the appropriate role for a consultant was to maintain objectivity and detachment, to be uninvolved in the client's issues. As I participated in subsequent training, and began to conduct training sessions as well, I was on my way to becoming a skilled professional manipulator (for other people's good, of course).

Then something happened. I had a crisis in my own life, and despite all my knowledge of behavioral science theory and techniques and my supposedly superior abilities in the realms of logic and rationality, I found myself totally unable to deal with my own dilemma. There was no satisfactory solution. Day after day and night after night, my mind boiled silently and ceaselessly, repeating the same involuted patterns of reasoning, but to no avail. It was no use; there was no solution. Yet there must be—there always had been before—so my mind churned anew.

Finally, I acknowledged that I needed help with my dilemma (although by this time, it was not a single dilemma, but more a restless collection of vague, half-formulated dissatisfactions). I explored a variety of physical and psychological remedies for my discontent. After a time, I was introduced to Gestalt, a school of psychology that focuses on increasing people's awareness of their environments, the clarity of their objectives, and their abilities to make choices about their actions.

As I worked with Gestalt psychologists and therapists, I began not only to learn, but to experience Gestalt theory's healing and growth-encouraging potential. My brief but intense crisis came to an end, or more accurately, evolved into a new set of ideas and feelings that for me felt good and satisfying, even exhilarating.

I experienced other changes as well. The range of my personal style expanded. I and others around me discovered (though I imagine they suspected it before) that I could be authoritarian, demanding, and blunt. I could also be warm, cooperative, and loving. Gradually, I became less self-restrained, more spontaneous, and sometimes less moderate. More willing to be seen for what I was and how I was. As best I could tell, some people liked me better this way and others less. I liked me better this way (though I confess that there were moments when I wasn't at all sure I did). What was clear was that the change felt right to me, and there was no going back.

As I became more familiar with the Gestalt notion of "first

dealing with the obvious," and as I became comfortable with a less meticulous regimen for working with clients, I would sometimes set aside the consulting model I had been taught. I temporarily gave up my concentration on diagnosing the organizational issue according to a standard "catalogue," identifying a remedial program, and planning an implementation process.

Instead, I focused on the client himself (almost all my clients at that time were male) and on the simple and direct—what he wanted and what he worried about or wanted to avoid. To encourage venturesome thinking, I asked him to extend his imagination to what he might achieve if he had all the power or influence or resources he would ever need. By jointly venturing beyond the constraints of conventional thinking, we often found more appealing goals that generated new energy and often also discovered previously unrecognized possible paths for achieving these goals.

Fundamental Principles

After a time, I found the principles and methods of the Gestalt approach to be germane to the everyday work of people in organizations, and later I joined with several others in developing and adapting Gestalt methods for use in organizations. My book *Authentic Management*, coauthored with Mike Korenich, was one result of that effort. Mike and I also conducted many workshops, and we and other consultants, particularly at the Gestalt Institute of Cleveland, used Gestalt methods extensively in work with clients.

A Force of Ones is based on the perspectives of the more than fifteen years I have spent consulting with and counseling managers since *Authentic Management* was published. In that time, of course, my views have continued to evolve, mostly in the direction of noticing and appreciating the broad spectrum of actions people take to survive and flourish in organizations. There are just many more of these actions than I first recognized. Nevertheless, many of the basics that Mike and I stated in *Authentic Management* remain as sharply valid now as they were then, and I have adapted them for *A Force of Ones*. The principles that follow are the drivers of the book.

• *Each individual is fundamentally in charge of his or her own life*, and try as we might, we can't escape that fact. We can join a support group and sympathize with each other or cheer each other along. We can take on responsibility for others. Others can take on responsibility for us. We can provide money, love, advice, or anything else to others, but eventually and ultimately, each of us has to make our own choices and take our own actions and chances.

• *All models are transient.* In physics, Galileo's model of the physical world was replaced by Newton's, Newton's by Einstein's, and now, Einstein's by quantum theory and subatomic physics. And there is no sign that the march of change in this field has ended. In sexual mores, we have moved in a much shorter time from Victorian concealment and inhibition to profuse explicitness and permissiveness. Management and organizational theories have also changed rapidly. As a result, since you cannot reasonably hope for a reliable, stable catalogue of organizational facts and prescriptions from which to draw your answers, you are going to have to bet your money and plunge

12

ahead. (Later, I discuss ways of tapping into your own internal resources of intuition, insight, and inspiration to help you better handle uncertainty and turbulence.)

• *Honesty is the best policy.* With apologies to William Shakespeare, I say, This above all, to thine own self be true; after that, you can lie or tell the truth to others, as you see fit. The honesty I am speaking of is not compulsive truth telling. It is a willingness to recognize your own biases and to occasionally reconsider them. It is not a full-scale assault on your belief system, but a gentle and gradual change that allows you to finish up with old habits and leftover introjections that no longer serve your purpose and to move on to new possibilities. Generally, I believe that our neglect, even evasion, of honesty in recent years has seriously blunted our ability as a society to deal with our most important problems. In politics and as members of groups (often well intentioned), we so carefully avoid possible offense to other groups that we never come to grips with core issues. Political correctness keeps us from sorting things out, from genuinely recognizing and bridging our differences. We cop out in our language with euphemisms and indirection. We think about other groups as monolithic and the people in them as all the same in their wants and points of view. We are so invested in our ideas about the categories to which we assign others that we block ourselves from seeing each other as singular persons. As actress Anna Devere Smith said in an interview, "Until you are willing to deal with me as an individual rather than a member of a minority I can't negotiate my own particular five-foot nine-inch, light-skinned blackness and who I really am. We have to talk to each other rather than about each other."

- *Personal development is a matter of filling in holes (wholes).* Each individual is a unique entity and each has his or her own particular set of capabilities and gaps. If you are articulate and aggressive, you may need to learn listening and receptivity. If you are passive and retiring, you may need to learn assertiveness. There is no single path or program that suits us all.

The almost exclusive promotion in recent years of group, team, and large-system thinking needs to be balanced by another view. Emphasizing group performance has resulted in consensus becoming the popular gospel. As preached by well-meaning advocates, the message is fit in to your group's effort. In practice, that often translates to don't rock the boat, or keep your head down. Individual visions and viewpoints are set aside in favor of a contribution to consensus. When your primary objective is to fit in to a congenial group effort, you work most at not standing out. Mediocrity is the perfect camouflage, and if you work at it long enough, you can eventually succeed in stifling that provocative inside voice that questions the consensus and churns out its own ideas and viewpoints.

This book and its author owe a great deal to many people and sources, especially to Frederick (Fritz) Perls. Perls, a tough-minded psychotherapist, believed that psychological analysis had its limitations. He believed that, after a point, analysis and conceptualizing contributed more to avoiding a problem or issue than to solving it. He believed that what was more useful was "finishing old business" and moving on to the new modes (see *Gestalt Therapy Verbatim* [1969]). He also thought that most people functioned best when they functioned in their natural styles, rather than according to someone else's model of what would be best for them. His view was that many of these models were based on "pluralistic ignorance" and represented "a set of things that nobody really believes in but everybody believes that everybody else believes in."

As author John Dos Passos (1920) wrote, "Individualism is each person's search for his own reality—a truth that he can know—not because he has been told by those in authority. Individuality is the capacity to stand alone, even in loneliness, without terror, without abject surrender to the collective view."

INDIVIDUALISM

If you think of your life
Your own personal life
As just an ordinary one,
A commonplace one
Without noteworthy excellences
Or faults

It isn't.
Your life is
A spectacular achievement
Full of unusual challenges
And heroic responses.

All lives are.
If you think that your abilities
Are best covered over and unnoticed
In the general mass of other people's abilities

They aren't.
You just haven't yet recognized them
Or valued them
Or learned to offer them.

Notes:
Reclaiming Individualism

- Individualism is neither selfish nor generous, domineering nor submissive. Those qualities are determined by personal character.

- Individualism means having a personal vision, recognizing your own ultimate authority for deciding what's right for you and your responsibility for living with the choices you make. Being in touch with your individuality increases your self-assurance, freedom, and personal power. You choose how you will use that freedom and power.

- At a fundamental level, the quality of all human organization's performance is the result of interactions between individuals. You can't build a great system from a collection of mediocre parts.

-

TAPPING INTO YOUR SINGULAR VISION

THIS BOOK'S AIM is to help you be better at what you do and enjoy it more. Later, I'll focus on how you can recognize and develop your own tailor-made versions of the skills you need to improve your effectiveness, power, and personal satisfaction. But there are prerequisites for that kind of change: first, you must really want to do it; and second, you must clear away the impediments in your way.

Part One (Chapters One through Five) focuses on recognizing and getting over, around, or through obstacles, particularly the kind you may put in your own path. It provides a number of methods and tools for discovering how you, *as an individual*, can sharpen your focus on what it is you want to accomplish, and sharpen your ability to make it happen. These chapters cover ways you can increase the effect of your participation and influence in basic interactions with others. They identify a more realistic perspective (as contrasted to the current mythology) of management work—namely, that despite the conventional planning-control view, management work is mainly a job of reacting to unforeseen demands. And they provide tools for becoming a more skillful reactor and for cutting through time-consuming rituals, identifying what's important and what's not, and tapping into your own and other people's energy and skills for making things happen.

Eight Ducking Games:
A Parable

ONE DAY, WHEN IT WAS RAINING and there weren't many people at the airport, a semi-wise man of ideas came to the Globaltech Company (which was and still is located in Organizationville). He was called a consultant, and he was semi-wise because he knew a lot about some things and was quite ignorant about some others, and he himself did not always know which was which. (If he had, he would have been a very wise man indeed.)

At the airport, the semi-wise man of ideas was met by a semi-wise man of action who was called an executive. After greeting each other and eating an expensive and somewhat too heavy lunch, which was the custom at such meetings, both semi-wise men returned to the large and elegant office of the semi-wise man of action and sat down to speak with each other.

"I am sorely troubled, consultant," said the executive, "and this is why I have sent for you from over many miles and borders."

"So I expected," replied the consultant wisely, and he peered over the tops of his eyeglasses and so appeared even wiser. "Tell me your dilemma, and I will listen."

"In my enterprise," said the executive, "are many managers and executives who must each day confront and decide upon many issues that come before them. If their decisions are good, the enterprise prospers. If they are poor, the enterprise suffers."

"So it is in many enterprises that I visit," said the consultant.

"True," said the executive, "but in Globaltech, there is another thing that happens, or more correctly, I must say, does not happen. For the managers and executives of this place too often make neither good nor poor decisions. Rather, they do not make decisions at all. And so the enterprise suffers as much as—and sometimes I fear more than—if the decisions had been poor. Tell me, consultant, if you know something about these matters that I may find useful."

The consultant replied, "I will speak to you of eight ducking games for executives, and you may judge if that is useful or not."

"That I will do," the executive said. "I pay you much for your counsel, and it is fitting that the words be useful."

Game 1

And so the consultant said, "The first game is called *More Data Needed*. It is a delicate game but not difficult to play. When there is a choice to be made between alternatives and that choice is not clear, the manager may say 'our information is inadequate,' or, 'we must wait until the trends are clearer,' or 'the staff work here is insufficient in quantity' or quality, or both. And so by playing More Data Needed, she may easily delay deciding."

"Ah, of course," exclaimed the executive, "I saw such a game played last week in one of our departments. I shall note it down so I will be alert to it the next time it is played."

Game 2

"The second game is called *It Never Should Have Happened in the First Place*," continued the consultant. "It is especially common when a manager faces difficult and unpleasant emergencies. When the manager cannot readily think of any attractive solution to the problem, he may say, 'If my predecessor [or my leader or whoever else may be convenient] had done his job more competently, this problem would never have arisen.' A variation of this game, which may be played between departments, is called *It's Not My Problem, It's Theirs*."

"Yes," sighed the executive, "I have certainly seen both versions played at Globaltech. It is not new to me, but I will note it anyway, so that I will be reminded."

Game 3

"*Power, Power, Who Has the Power* is the third game," said the consultant, "and it is most often played in committees and advisory groups. When action must be taken that requires some departure from standard procedures or a change in conventional policies, committee members may say, 'Yes, I think it would be a good idea, but it would take somebody higher up to swing it,' or, 'We might do that except no one in this group has the authority.' This game, by the way, may be played at any level in the organization. I have seen vice presidents who were most skilled at it, and while I have never witnessed it, I expect that chief executives play a version too."

"This game, too, I have heard about, indirectly," said the executive rather quickly. "I'll make a note of it while you tell me about the fourth game."

Game 4

"The fourth game is known as *Waver*," said the consultant, "and it, too, is most often played in meetings. Waver is a subtle game and requires more skill and precise timing than most. It has the advantage, though, of being visible only to the keenest eyes. The object is for a group that wishes to avoid making a decision to cycle back and forth between two or more alternatives without ever coming to a conclusion. The test of skill, of course, is to see how close to a decision the group can come and still not quite make one. Thus to the observer, and at times to the group members themselves, their deliberations appear cogent and relevant, except at the final instant when they switch to a reverse track. Championship-calibre Waver players may make this game last for weeks, even months."

"Hmm," said the executive. "I remember a meeting of my division heads in which they discussed investment but never quite completed their discussion. If I am not mistaken, they were playing Waver then. I'll jot this one down as well."

Game 5

"*What Will Harry Think?*" continued the consultant, "is the name of ducking game number 5. It is a very simple game that may be played by any number of players and needs no special setting. When courage or trust is low among executives and anxiety or suspicion is high, a course of action may be delayed, at least for a short while, by worrying about what Harry would think. Harry may be a superior or a peer. And no one, of course, takes the trouble to ask Harry what he actually thinks, for that would defeat the game's purpose. Instead, the players speculate on his reactions and so find many reasons to avoid reaching a conclusion. If the players wish to extend the game, options are available. For once the question of what Harry would think is answered, the players can ask what Martha, Roy, and Jennifer would think as well."

"Yes, indeed," smiled the executive, "and Peter and Paul and Saint Sebastian, too. I have seen this game played often, and it has just as often annoyed me." And he added the fifth game to his list.

Game 6

"The sixth game is called *Yeah, but...*, and it is frequently a competitive game," the consultant remarked. "It is played in two strokes. Player 1 proposes an idea or a solution to a problem, and his opponent, player 2, responds, 'Yeah, but...,' and then fills in the reasons why the idea or solution won't work or is inadequate or has been tried before and failed. The game is often played by in-group members in response to ideas proposed by nonmembers. If it is played well, those in the in-group can successfully resist the penetration of any new ideas.

"Another interesting version of this game is played most often by those who ask for others' advice even though they are determined not to change their present course. As advice is given by player 2 in response to player 1's apparently sincere request, player 1 Yeah, buts... each contribution. With skill, player 1 may frustrate several advisors simultaneously or sequentially and then walk away complaining sadly that no one in the world can solve his problem. This result, of course, makes his problem a very superior one compared to the run-of-the-mill variety most of us have."

"Well," observed the executive, "that is another game with which I am only too familiar, in both versions. There are two divisions in this enterprise that constantly Yeah, but... each other's proposals and have done so for years. Also, we have a controller who is exactly like your example of player 1. I myself have tried to help him many times. I certainly want to list this game."

Game 7

"The seventh game," said the consultant, "is a sad one. It is called, *Wash Out*, and it may be played by a single player or a group. It is usually played when there is a lack of confidence in a person or an organization and sometimes when there is a lack of hope. The game goes like this: An individual (or group) faces a problem or challenge to be met and develops an idea or approach. But unlike player 1 in the Yeah, but... game, she does not wait for an opponent to contest the worth of the concept. Instead she does it herself. Wash Out is the game of self-defeat that is lost before it has even begun."

"I have seen it too in Globaltech," said the executive, "and my heart has been heavy. As I watched it played, I wished there was something I could have done," and he noted down game 7.

"Before I describe game 8," said the consultant, "there is something I would like to ask."

"Yes?" The executive glanced up curiously from his list, "What is it?"

"I would like to know your judgment of the usefulness of those things I have so far told you. Has what I have said of the seven games been worth the amount you pay me?"

"That is a difficult question to answer," replied the executive after several moments' thought. "Your explanation of the games has been interesting and well put, though I must say that most of these things I knew before, and in truth, I see the games played almost every day." The semi-wise man of action paused to ponder. "Yes, I must admit I am hard put at this moment to say whether you have been worth your fee or not. Perhaps your explanation of the eighth and last game will tip the scales one way or the other."

Game 8

"Very well," said the semi-wise man of ideas, "I will continue. The eighth game is the game of *Consultant*. It is usually played only by those who are high up in an enterprise, for only they can afford to play it. Consultant may be a useful game if it is not played too often or too long, but when it is played as a substitute for doing what needs to be done, it is not at all useful. Consultant, after all, is a game of talking and listening and not a game of doing. Therefore, sir," the consultant leaned close to the executive as he spoke, "my words and your notes of them may

27

indeed be interesting and well put, but if you do no more with them than you have so far with your own experiences of them, Consultant will be a no better game than any of the previous seven."

The executive smiled. "Now I will answer your question," he said. "What you have told me is indeed worth the price."

When the semi-wise man of ideas left the semi-wise man of action at the airport on the following day, the rain had stopped and while the clouds were still dark and rolled heavily above them, on the horizon was a small but clear streak of blue.

CHAPTER ONE

Getting Out of Your Own Way

THIS BOOK ASPIRES to stimulate *singular* visions and to support the initiative and determination of exceptional individuals, like you, who are willing to discover themselves and to work at times in isolation and at other times in voluntary combination to achieve extraordinary purposes. Such achievement is not always easy. Obstacles get in the way. Sometimes other people put them there; more often you put them there yourself, or you collude with others, in games similar to the eight just described. You and others talk about these games as "part of the culture," and of course, you, a single individual, can't fight the culture alone. Or can you?

Reluctance to risk standing out is understandable. Sometimes, long-held attitudes and beliefs you have about yourself and others can be powerful inhibitors to discovering and using your own power and talents. Other times, it's a matter of not having the skills and methods to make your force felt. In this chapter, I'll describe some typical obstacles and ways of getting through, around, or over them.

Clarifying Your Own Boundaries

You sit with others around a conference table, afraid to say what you think, trying to figure out if the sides have been chosen, and if so, who is on which side, and which side you ought to join. There has been a great deal of talk, but you don't quite know what it has been about because you have been too busy figuring.

You have been called on to make a presentation to a group of higher-echelon managers. You wish you were somewhere else, anywhere else. Your mouth is dry and your palms wet. How, you wonder, can you make your case in a way that won't make you look foolish?

For those with no clear sense of their own boundaries in both business and personal situations, the questions always are, What do *they* expect? What is the *right* way? What are *they* thinking? What would *they* like to hear? And this merry-go-round of speculation about what *they* are thinking and what you should say or do to please *them* accomplishes nothing except increasing your anxiety.

An individual may be a member of any number of communities, a participant in any number of groups, a subscriber to any number of viewpoints, and a believer in any number of philosophies, and still know that he or she was born, is living, and will die within his or her own skin. The boundary of *your* self is, in a very literal sense, *your* skin. The boundary of *my* self is *my* skin. I am, therefore, at least potentially, the world's greatest expert on me. You are, or can be, the greatest expert on you. Neither of us really knows what goes on inside the other's skin. We can imagine it, we can guess at it, but we can't really know.

But our skins are not merely unfeeling walls that surround and imprison us, for they contain our sensing apparatuses.

Your sense of touch is your means for feeling what is outside yourself, your eyes are your way of seeing what is outside, your ears your way of hearing what is outside, and so on. Thus, your physical boundaries are not only your limits, they are also your means for coming in contact with other people and things in your world. When you have a clear sense of not only your physical boundaries but also your mental and emotional boundaries and can distinguish thoughts, emotions, and wants that are yours and those that belong to others, you are less likely to filter another person's communication through the often distorting screens of your speculations and conjectures, as the executives did while playing the eight ducking games I described earlier.

When your self-boundaries are blurred, you typically become confused about where your thoughts and impressions end and others' begin. Often the people who have clouded or blurred their boundaries do so in the mistaken belief that only by abdicating their individuality, their distinctive thoughts and feelings, can they make themselves acceptable to others. To be accepted, they must be like others. People may be willing to do this for the sake of finding security in the group. Unfortunately, it can be a poor bargain. The security they buy is often neither satisfying nor reliable. The quest to find identification and safety in others can produce a backlash: feelings of insignificance and low self-esteem, suspicions that other people influence you too much and can't be relied upon for support, or resentment that others place their own interests before yours.

The consequences of blurred self-boundaries can multiply themselves. When both you and those you engage have blurred boundaries, then both you and they are seeking the "right" things to say and do, searching for the secret formula. As a result, there's no solidity or commitment between you and them, nor is there much likelihood that anyone will come away from the encounter well satisfied. There has been no genuine exchange between human beings who are willing to state where they stand and what they want. You have not reviewed each other's positions and desires to see where they are compatible and where they are not, and have not made solid arrangements with one another about what to do. Thus, the outcomes of these blurred encounters are also blurred.

Clear self-boundaries encourage the development of self-support within an individual, rather than a dependence on group supports. Working within a group, sharing its efforts, problems, and both tangible and intangible rewards are all worthwhile activities. But so are asserting your position, negotiating, compromising, or dissenting.

A good sense of your own boundaries can provide you with what is often called inner strength. People who have a sound sense of their self-boundaries are often good people to be around. They tend to be competent, clear about both their strengths and weaknesses, easy to communicate with, and open with others. They are also more likely to seem sure of themselves, a quality that may at times annoy those who are less sure.

Individuals who are clear about their self-boundaries are less likely to occupy the extreme ends of the personal power spectrum, less prone to suffer from an omnipotence syndrome (overestimating their effect on others) or from an impotence syndrome (feeling incapable of influencing their own fate). Individuals with a good sense of their own boundaries can listen to people with large reputations and people with small ones, to people who speak loudly and those who speak softly, but neither reputation nor volume determines what strong individuals will believe. They listen to others' opinions and ideas with minimal defensiveness and distortion of the incoming information. They are confident that, ultimately, they will not be influenced beyond the degree to which they wish to accept influence. They are in charge of themselves.

Avoiding and Diluting Communication

Good contact with others grows out of your being fully present in and sharply aware of your environment. When you are not making good contact, your senses are disrupted and you and the others involved are distracted. You may be busy worrying about the outcome of the meeting, winning a point, or maintaining your image or playing out your idea of the "right" role. You are certainly thinking of something other than what's going on in your immediate vicinity.

Discussion in which good contact is made often has a personal quality—the people conversing are interested in the subject matter they're talking about, and in what others have to say. They're not just going through a conversational ritual. Next time you're at a meeting, a party, or some other gathering, stop for a minute and listen to the sounds. It isn't hard to distinguish the lively, even excited sounds of good contact from those of people who are avoiding connecting.

There are certainly times when people, sometimes for good

reason, choose to avoid connecting. Contact often leads to action, influence, or involvement with another person, and there are times when all you want to do is be polite. Often, though, a missed contact is unintended, the result of habitual ineffective communication patterns. Two common examples of such patterns are *abstract discourse* and *self-dilution*.

Abstract Discourse

Abstract discourse is easy to recognize. People deliver lectures or make speeches at each other; often, they seem to bounce these speeches off the farthest wall, or worse, just let them drop into the middle of the room. When they speak, it may be to the carpet or the ceiling, but one thing is sure, it is not to each other. For example, at a staff meeting the foreman, face blank, seems to study the floor as he says, "One of the problems with the engineering approach of this division is that the designs tend to be too complicated to be producible." Yet he is actually speaking to the engineer, and what he means is, "My crew is having a helluva time producing this new product your organization has passed on to us. I would appreciate it if you would see if you can redesign the process."

The foreman may be avoiding contact for a number of reasons. If he is not entirely sure of his case, he may be fearful of a counterattack. He may imagine that if he made his request directly the engineer would be offended and react negatively. What the foreman doesn't realize is that his message of dissatisfaction probably comes through anyway, though in an ambiguous form, while the indirectness of his complaint makes it unlikely that corrective action will be taken. The indirectness makes it difficult for the engineer to respond, and he may counter with similar indirectness or avoid the subject entirely. If this goes on long enough, both the foreman and the engineer will likely develop a secret discomfort with each other that will be an obstacle both to themselves and the organization. I've known resentments to exist for years between members of an organization, never explicitly dealt with and forever interfering with their interactions.

Self-Dilution

Diluting a message is another common way in which people undermine the force of their communication. Self-diluting is usually accomplished by making a statement about the way you see a situation, but then qualifying your point sufficiently to wash out its impact. A general manager says to her marketing director, "Bill, I'm not sure that our percentage of the market, especially in the new customer segment, is as good as it might be. Now, of course, I realize you've had staffing problems, and general business conditions haven't been too good, but still, maybe we should have concentrated more on our West Coast regions, though I know we did some of that last year."

On the face of it, the general manager's statement seems fair-minded, and she appears to be an understanding person. However, it is hard for the marketing director to read the general manager's message. Is she concerned about the percentage of new customers or not? The complaint, if there is one, is never quite made and so can't be dealt with. If the general manager is indeed ambivalent and merely musing out loud, then she is not asking for a response or for follow-up action (and she is not likely to get it). If, however, she is trying to be delicate about voicing a serious concern, that concern is unlikely to be heard.

35

Self-dilution is one way that those who are uncomfortable with their power mute the expression of that power. Some people are taught at an early age that power is bad. Others have concerns about wounding other people's feelings, making others mad, or being completely fair or accurate. In fact, as I will discuss later, power is neither good nor bad. It's just there, and if you don't claim your share, someone else will be glad to claim it.

For other people, self-dilution is a defense strategy—no one can criticize or disappoint you much when you haven't taken a stand. As the inept door-to-door salesman said to his prospect, "You wouldn't want to buy a vacuum cleaner from me, would you?" The problem is that those who are prone to criticizing will criticize you whether you take a stand or not.

Use the following two checklists to assess your own contact and message-sending practices. The first list deals with making contact with other people. However, you and I also need to make contact with issues. Therefore, the second list checks how well we have succeeded in addressing the ideas that we wanted to communicate.

Self-Checklist
for Contact with Others

The best way to use this list is to apply it to a particular interaction in which you were recently involved. If you like, apply the exercise to several interactions and score yourself on a scale of 1 to 5 on each item. Add up your scores to identify your communication patterns and opportunities for improvement.

1. Did I talk abstractly or generalize rather than dealing with the issue squarely?

36

2. Did I say, "I can't," when what I really meant was I don't want to?
3. Did I ask rhetorical questions, pretending that I was looking for information, when what I really wanted to do was make a statement?
4. Did I deliver discourses or talk about the past when the issue was important in the present?
5. Was I clear about where I stand on an issue—saying no when I meant no, and yes when I meant yes?
6. Did I stop when I had made my point, or did I dilute my point by continuing on and on with examples and anecdotes?
7. Did I "broadcast" into the air, the rug, or the group in general rather than talk directly to the person(s) that I wanted to reach?
8. Did I really see and hear what was going on, or did I think about the future or the past, or imagine what someone else might have been thinking?

Self-Checklist
for Contact with Issues

Use the following supplementary questions to define your relations to particular issues with which you may currently be dealing.

1. Am I dealing with the real problem or an abstraction of it? (For example, is it a communication problem or is it that Joe is really so insistent on getting his own way that he can't be moved?)
2. Do I intend to do anything about this issue, or am I just going through the motions?

3. Is more information going to help or just delay the resolution? Do I need to make a choice now? What are the costs of waiting?
4. Am I stuck in a swamp of old answers, or am I willing to consider something new?
5. Does this problem belong to me, or am I renting it?
6. Am I spending too much time second-guessing what my boss and others would consider the right answer?

Introjection — Swallowing Without Chewing

Introjection starts in early childhood. You might call it a swallowing whole of other people's ideas, judgments, or styles. An example is the table manners that you and I absorbed when we were children. Kids introject elaborate behavioral models, especially from parents, teachers, older kids, and even from their sports heroes. You can probably remember some time in your life (maybe just yesterday) when you found yourself walking, talking, or otherwise imitating the style of someone you admired — without being aware of it until someone pointed out the resemblance to you.

Many introjections are harmless and even fun. They last for a while and then are replaced by new ones or just go away. Others, though, are less transient. They can become substitutes for your own thinking and feeling. Sometimes, they can keep you from finding your best path through an issue or opportunity. Some children introject large chunks of their parents' value systems in ways that seriously interfere with the children's later ability to lead satisfying lives of their own — for example, the man who keeps himself from a warm and full relationship with any woman because he has introjected his father's distrust and suspicion of women and their motives, or the woman who drives herself to exhaustion and frustration at work because she has introjected her father's ambition. The point, of course, is not that the first father's suspicion and the second father's ambition are inappropriate in themselves. The first father may have had personal cause to be suspicious, and the second to be ambitious, but each lived in a different time and led a different life than his children, and what may have been right for the fathers as individuals may not be right for their offspring as individuals.

Problems with Organizational Introjections

At the office, laboratory, or plant, introjecting continues as people gulp role models such as the Perfect Manager. A perfect manager makes quick decisions and appears decisive and self-assured at all times. She has a continuing interest in her team and communicates with them fully. She solicits their participation and leads them to consensus decisions. A perfect manager also wears the company hat rather than being unduly influenced by the interests of her own department or her future career. And so on.

The big problem with introjections is that the people who gulp them hardly ever fully digest them. If you haven't truly chewed your introjections enough so that your personal system can separate out what's nutritious for you from what is not, the whole thing becomes a big undigested lump that eventually gives you emotional heartburn. You keep insisting to yourself that you ought to follow the perfect manager's principles, but you never live up to your intention because the intention doesn't match the way you are. What if your personal decision-making

39

style is slow and deliberate rather than quick? What if there are times when you are *not* sure of yourself? And what if, in actual fact, you are more concerned at the moment with your own career progress than with either your employees' comfort or the company's big picture?

Introjections can get in the way of your recognizing your own current internal realities and accepting them as reasonable ways of feeling. When your introjections do get in your way, you can get caught up in denials, contradictions, and rationalizations that further obscure the actual scene.

Moreover, when people finally do react against their introjections, they sometimes find themselves rejecting not only the indigestible parts but also the useful and appropriate parts. A manager who had introjected his boss's super aggressive style attended a management training program and came to the conclusion that he should adopt a less directive, more facilitative style (a new introjection). On returning to work, he resolved to run his organization by consensus. In dealing with some issues, however, he found that his subordinates were restricted in their views by their lack of knowledge about their industry's changing economics in the face of increasing European competition. Fortunately, as time went by, his good sense helped him to moderate his style to include both facilitation and directiveness.

Training the Operational You

When you try to adopt prescriptions that don't suit you, you seldom do it well. Your subordinates and peers, and others, can often sense the incongruity. The role you play seems out of line with the other signals you simultaneously send. If you say to your subordinates, "I'd like all of us to discuss this policy issue and come to a consensus on what to do about it," and at the same time, you sit on the edge of your chair, peek at your watch every minute or so and grind your teeth, your subordinates may think twice about venturing ideas that require leisurely consideration.

The management style that is right for you needs to be tailor-made, and the tailor has to be you. The point is not that training programs for managers are useless. Many programs provide ideas and techniques that are well worth considering—but not introjecting.

Management training that promotes one "best" model of managing has limited usefulness. Fortunately, a fair number of contemporary approaches to training fall under the "contingency," or "situational," management philosophy, which states that the right way to manage is determined by a combination of factors including task complexity, employee maturity, and organizational culture. These contemporary approaches are clearly more effective than their predecessors. Even so, they all require consideration of an additional factor: the operational characteristics of the individual manager.

Training the operational you requires some toughness of mind. It is not inordinately difficult, but the best way to proceed requires getting beyond the business of judging yourself, especially in overly indulgent ways ("Ain't I great?" or "Ain't I awful?"). If you don't approve of some of the ways you operate, you can work at changing them. This book can provide useful assistance. But in the meantime, don't waste time criticizing

41

or punishing yourself. When you are working to improve the functioning of single individuals in the long and complex chain of organizational structures, you must start at the top of the chain—with yourself. That's a force of one.

No one grants you freedom,
You are free if you are free.

No one enthralls you,
You enthrall yourself
And when you have
You may hand your tether
   to another,
   to many others,
   to all others, or
   to yourself.

Perhaps this last is worst of all.
For this slave master is hardest to see
And hardest to rebel against
But easiest to hate and to damage.

I do not know how to tell you to be free,
I wish I did.
But I do know some signs of freedom—
One is in doing what you want to do
   though someone tells you not to.
Another is in doing what you want to
   though someone tells you to.

Notes:
Getting Out of Your Own Way

- Each person is born, lives, and will die within his or her own skin. Your personal boundaries distinguish you from all other people, *and* they are the means by which you make contact with others, as one human being to another.

- You have clear self-boundaries when you know which ideas and feelings are yours and which belong to others. When your boundaries are clear, you are better able to appreciate the ideas and feelings of others without sentimental or defensive distortions, because you are in charge of yourself.

- Membership in groups, organizations, and cultures is a part of human social life; but if you rely on membership for your identification and group support for your security, you will inevitably be disappointed. When your self-boundaries are clear, you participate in your community but are not submerged by it.

- If you don't claim your share of power, someone else will. Talking in generalizations or abstractions, avoiding contact and engagement, and excessively qualifying your messages are habits that diminish your power and influence.

- There is no single best model of managerial behavior (or any other behavior). Your style must fit your character and take advantage of your natural strengths. When you try to adapt yourself to prescriptions that don't fit, others often sense the incongruity and do not trust you.

-

CHAPTER TWO

Interactions That Get Things Done

IN A SHINY-FLOORED, brightly lit corridor seven floors down from the Globaltech boardroom, Jill Chevrier walks slowly. Her head hurts and her shoulders slump as she struggles back to her cubicle in a haze of frustration. It happened again. This was her third two-hour session with Ralph Bradley, the division purchasing manager, and nothing has been decided. By Jill's estimate, finalizing the vendor list for the new software system should have been wrapped up in three meetings, but she and Ralph were barely started on it. Somehow, they kept wandering off onto paths that went nowhere.

Ralph always seemed to be pecking for more details than necessary and reciting anecdotes about the company's good old days. Some were interesting and a few funny, but all drained valuable time. So far, the discussions had been like a maze. They reminded Jill of the story of the stranger asking the old New Englander for directions to Bangor. "Well, son," the old man said after sucking his pipe for a while, "don't rightly think you can get there from here."

Jill couldn't hold herself blameless. She had slogged through enough assertiveness-training sessions to know that she was

45

responsible for her actions and for making her views known. Yet she didn't feel that she had anything to be assertive about. Ralph was not domineering; in fact, he was rather shy. The problem was that neither of them seemed to be able to stay on the subject. They didn't lack ideas. Ideas were what led them around the maze, through one blind pathway after another. They needed to find the highway that would take them home to a decision.

Getting Better at Basic Interactions

This chapter is about the basics of effective interaction. An interaction is effective when you and one or more other people

- Reach agreements that all parties understand in the same way
- Are committed to taking follow-up action on those agreements
- Have positive feelings about doing business together

The approach I recommend has two underlying biases. The first bias is in favor of honesty. It says that *straightforwardness is the shortest and most reliable distance between you and the other person.* The second bias says that *when an interaction is not going the way you want it to, you have the option of changing it through your own behavior.* Whether you use that option or not is up to you. Part of what individualism is about is owning your power and making choices.

Don't forget though that workability is more important than a grand gesture. I'm not preaching sudden conversions. You travel this road at your own pace. This chapter describes the five steps that are all you need to lead or take part in interactions that get things done rather than just talked about. The process works whether your interaction is with one person or a number of them.

Jill isn't alone in her frustration. The number of business people lost in go-nowhere discussion mazes increases daily. As products become more complex, organizations become more complicated and so do people's interactions. The typical dead ends are not hard to spot, and they happen in two-person discussions as well as in larger gatherings. Recognize them?

- *The mystery.* You walk into a meeting without knowing its purposes and by meeting's end you're not any clearer.

- *The never-ending circle.* You sit through sessions in which many people say many words but little progress is made toward a conclusion.

- *The slipped knot.* You come away from a discussion with what you think is an agreement, only to discover later that the other person had a significantly different understanding.

- *The forgotten promise.* You wait for an agreement to be implemented, but someone fails to follow up with the action required to bring the agreement into effect.

The Five C's for Better Interactions

If you have been involved in so many of these conversational mazes that you're wondering if there's any alternative, take

47

heart. There is. There are five simple steps to escaping the maze. You can easily remember them as the five C's: contact, contract, concreteness, checking, and closing. They build a framework for communicating with others in more satisfying ways. With the five C's, you can accomplish more in less time with clearer outcomes, good feelings, and mutual commitment to follow up. Your interactions will be civil and considerate, but they will also have a new directness and sense of purpose.

1. Contact: Getting in Touch

People make contact when they literally see, hear, and pay real attention to each other. Instead of launching yourself, rocket-like, at the issue, you and the other person take a minute to recognize each other as living human beings, not just pieces of equipment. This step is more than a courtesy. Good contact brings with it a higher than ordinary level of rapport, which usually broadens the avenues available for reaching agreement. Spending five minutes on contact at the beginning of a discussion may save you fifty minutes later on.

It's often helpful early in a meeting to share something that's on your mind or in your awareness. Nothing heavy, just something like, "I ran into some traffic on the way over here," or, "I like the view you have out this window." To the extent you're comfortable with doing it, you can also say something about your attitude toward the meeting: "I'm looking forward to this session with you," or, "I have some concerns about this session."

Contact ought to be renewed every once in a while when sessions are long. Taking a break from the action to step out of your role as manager, subordinate, or departmental representative and to share your thoughts and feelings about the meeting

48

so far often encourages reciprocal contact from the other person. Good contact builds trust between people and encourages them to get into real issues quicker and with less suspicion of each other.

How to make contact:

- Look at (but don't stare at), recognize, and listen to the other person.

- Exchange a few words about each other or some other subject of mutual interest.

- If this meeting is a follow-up to an earlier discussion, take a few minutes to summarize in a neutral way the main points each person made in the previous meeting. Show that you heard and appreciated what the other person said (even if you do not agree with what was said).

"Good to see you again," says Jill at her next meeting with Ralph. She notices that he has bright blue eyes, and there are worn-in laugh-lines around his mouth. "Ralph, I told my boss your story about the start-up of the semiconductor division, and he could hardly stop laughing." She notices that she has his attention. Jill then listens graciously to one more of Ralph's yarns before driving politely but firmly forward to the next step of purposeful interaction.

If you try making contact and get no reciprocation, wait a while and try again. If you still don't get an appropriate response, don't tighten up. Do the best you can and get on with business. The other person may open up to contact later. However, person-to-person contact is always a two-way road. Unless you are exceptionally sensitive, well grounded, and enjoy unusual ego strength, you probably can't maintain good contact with someone who doesn't want to be in contact with you. A few people do not like contact at all. It's uncomfortable for them. Even people who enjoy contact have times when they either feel too busy for it (that shouldn't be a frequent excuse) or just not in the mood.

To practice and appreciate good contact, you also have to practice and appreciate the other side of the coin—good withdrawal. It is unlikely that either you or I could tolerate being constantly in contact. For one thing, contact is often an exciting, involving experience, and it both generates and uses a good deal of energy. For another thing, good contact is also self-limiting—that is, good contact tends to produce action that allows you to finish the business that needs to be completed. With the completion of the business comes a natural reduction of the need for contact. As the need for contact and involvement diminishes, you may want a pause and some relaxation, or your attention may shift to another focus.

2. Contract: Knowing What Is to Be Accomplished

An interaction contract focuses on *the task, problem, or opportunity under consideration; what each party wants; and what each is willing to do*. In most interactions it won't be a written document. Rather, it's more likely to be one or two explicit proposals and agreements about the purposes for the meeting. (Posting some key words from those agreements on a blackboard can remind you and the other person to keep on track.) What happens when you don't develop those agreements and focus on them is illustrated by the communication dead ends, tangents, and slippages I described earlier.

In developing a set of mutual agreements, there are two objectives to consider:

- The final product or output you and the others want to achieve
- The goals for this particular meeting

For example, conferees from the research and development and the production departments may agree on the long-term objective of improving their process for transferring technology. They then may agree that the objective of their first meeting will be to agree on all the points at which the transfer process is currently unsatisfactory.

There are times when concise contracting becomes difficult. Sometimes, the issues aren't clear. For example, something isn't working well in a process or an interface between two people or departments, but it's not clear what the difficulty is. In this case, contracting probably ought to concentrate first on developing a list of possibilities, perhaps using a brainstorming technique. In the next meeting, contracting might focus on prioritizing that list.

Some interests or concerns may seem awkward to talk about—for example, concerns about the effects of particular decisions on a meeting participant's personal status or the standing of his or her department. When that's the case, work your way patiently toward recognizing and including these concerns. Good contact will make that easier to do.

How to make a contract:

- Take time to develop a clear and reasonably specific understanding about what you and the other participant want to see happen. Don't assume the outcome is too obvious to discuss. The picture in your mind may be different from your co-worker's picture.

- If the issue is complex or potentially controversial, it can be useful to share ideas about anticipated obstacles or other concerns.

- The contract need not be formal or rigid, but rather a mutually agreed to, provisional statement of direction. It can be changed if and when you and the other participants agree on an approach that better serves all your needs.

Jill and Ralph settle down now. She taps her pen lightly against the desk, and says, "With your permission, I would like to make a proposal." Ralph nods agreement, and Jill continues, "I think it would be useful if each of us started this session with a short statement about what we would like to accomplish in the meeting." She waits, and when there is no objection, she says, "Starting with myself, I believe our overall objective is to identify a sufficient number of approved vendors for each component in our RW-6 system. By the end of today's meeting I would like us to have produced a list of all the vendors we have full confidence in and all of those we have reasonable doubts about. I think that will help us focus on the next steps we need to take." When she finishes speaking, Jill waits attentively for Ralph to speak. She is going to listen closely.

3. Concreteness: Making It Simple and Specific

Being concrete means moving discussions down the abstraction ladder, converting broad or ambiguous statements and concepts into more specific information. For example, describing apparent difficulties between two departments as a "communications problem" is less useful than describing *who* is having a problem communicating *what, to whom,* and *under what circumstances.*

A general manager sent a memo to his human resource director that said, "John, what I'm wondering about is whether the Human Resources organization is a suitable function within which to incorporate our affirmative action program. Perhaps the circumstances and special requirements of these minority issues ought to be placed in a separate function." The HR director was disappointed and perplexed by the message.

Some days later, I was asked to assist at a face-to-face meeting between these two managers. We followed the five C's guidelines. After good contact had been established between the managers, the general manager was willing to be concrete and his statement became, "John, I'm not sure if you have the clout to give this company a strong affirmative action thrust. I think whoever does this job will need to push on some of us, including me, and you don't seem to be doing much of that lately."

Contact and concreteness are not always easy or entirely pleasant, but they're necessary if we are to know where each of us stands, and then take actions that address real issues rather than synthetic ones. In this particular case, some lively discussion followed about specific instances and the causes of the HR director's apparent avoidance of confrontations. It turned out that the HR director had backed off from controversy because he had believed that was what the general manager wanted him to do. In further conversation, the two reached a new agreement about the future orientation of both the director and his organization. The affirmative action program was placed within the HR organization.

Efforts to make an issue concrete should not be premature. In the early stages of discussion, exploring broad approaches can be useful, but at later stages, translating these approaches into sharply focused and simply stated particulars is important. Asking the following questions can help you achieve this focus:

- What is unsatisfactory about the current situation?
- What, specifically, does each party want to see changed?
- What is each party willing to do?

How to be concrete:

- Ask and answer the who, what, when, where, and how questions. (Notice that I didn't include *why*. There are usually too many reasons why.) It's not enough to agree generally that some action needs to be taken. Participants need to decide *who will do what, by when.*
- If a large, complex program is to be implemented, reduce it to a series of smaller, simpler action steps to power your program to its destination.

Ralph leans back in his chair and clasps his hands behind his balding head. "The reason why we can't use Avery Electronics as a vendor is simple. The problem is their management," he says.

Jill sips from her now almost cold coffee and waits for further details. When he speaks no further, she says, "Ralph, it would help me if you tell me more about that. What things about their management bother you, and how will their management affect the product quality or delivery we would get from them?"

4. Checking: Confirming the Direction

Checking is the process of taking a time-out for measurement. You and your colleague need to pause periodically at convenient places in the discussion to ask, How well are we doing at our joint task? *Are we doing what we set out to do in our contract?* If not, should we get back to that objective, or should we change the contract? You can also check how satisfied participants are with the way in which they are conducting the discussions. Is everyone getting the opportunity to express their views, and are people listening well to each other?

How to check:

- Prearrange one or two time-outs at the start of the meeting.

- Set a ground rule that allows any participant to call a time-out when he or she feels the discussion is off track.

- Measure individual satisfaction during the meeting. For instance, ask participants to raise one, two, or three fingers according to how satisfied they are with progress so far. Then ask for suggestions to improve the way you and the others are working together.

- When you check participant satisfaction don't dwell on what people are doing wrong. Instead, focus on what they want *more* of, *less* of, or *differently* from one another.

It is about halfway through the scheduled time of their session, and Jill and Ralph have just concluded a first-pass list of acceptable sources. It has not been easy. Each of them held some strong opinions, and there have been several disagreements, as well as some compromises. Feeling the time is right for a check,

Jill says, "I think it would be useful now for us to stop and take a reading on our progress. My own impression is that even though each of us has a few reservations, this list pretty well represents our consensus. What do you think?"

Ralph is not quite ready to commit fully. He asks for a day in which to discuss a few of the vendors further with his staff. Jill agrees. When that is settled, Jill says, "I would also like us to take another few minutes to check out how we feel about the way we have been working on this project so far. Are there any things you would like to see us do more of, less of, or differently, Ralph?"

5. Closing: Wrapping It Up

Closing is the very important last stop on the purposeful interaction track. It is the place to make decisions and commit to action. Closing enables the individuals in the work group to do a final check of whether they are satisfied that they have successfully concluded their business together. To close, participants review what has been achieved compared to the latest version of the contract and identify what, if anything, needs follow-up action. This closing "ceremony" also provides a vehicle for people to reinforce their contact with each other before going their separate ways. A good ending for the present interaction encourages a good beginning for the next one.

How to check: Good closure calls for the participants to answer these questions:

- Is there anything further we can do to assure success for the product or output as it moves to the next stage?

- What action items do each of us have? Who will do what, by when?

- Which items are undecided and what, if anything, needs to be done about them?

After these questions are answered, a last review of the group's interactions together can be useful, emphasizing accomplishments and satisfactions and how the interaction can improve next time. Finally, participants can take a moment or two to congratulate each other on a job well done.

When she finishes reading out the list of action items she and Ralph have agreed to, Jill squeezes the cap of her pen closed contentedly. "Well," she says, "I suppose that wraps it up. Is there anything else you can think of?" Ralph treats Jill to a broad grin, a rarity for him. "One thing. Since we do seem to have the opportunity to express ourselves here, I just wanted to say that we made a heck of a team," he says. "I hope we get a chance to work together again soon."

"I do too," Jill says, and she means it.

Grounding Yourself: Getting Settled and Set

Grounding is the foundation of effective interaction. When you are grounded, you are better able to stay calm and focused on the five C's. Your calm and focus are often communicated to the others involved and encourage a reciprocal attitude, making the interaction less hectic and more satisfying. So, before an important meeting or presentation, or anytime your pressure gauge begins to climb past the comfort zone, find a quiet spot and sit down and go through the following grounding process:

- Close your eyes (leave them half open if you'd rather), and loosen any tight clothing.

- Feel your feet on the floor and your buttocks on the chair. Keep your spine straight and relaxed, shoulders and head level.

- Patiently, one area at a time (feet, ankles, lower legs, and so on), check your body for tensions. Wherever you find tension, intensify it for a few moments, then let it go.

- Don't forget to breathe!

- After you've checked the top of your head, go back for a moment to feeling the ground under your feet again and the chair under your buttocks. Notice how you feel overall. Don't make a big thing out of the change, just make sure your mind and body get a good chance to experience themselves fully. Set your self-boundaries by reminding yourself, "Here I am." After that, get right back to business.

After you have practiced grounding for a while and become familiar with the feeling, you'll be able to ground yourself very quickly—within seconds.

Before meeting with the project committee to present the vendor list recommendations, Jill closes the door to her office, scoots off her shoes, and sits erect but comfortable in her chair. She becomes aware of her breathing and allows it to settle into a relaxed rhythm. She lets her eyes close and focuses her attention on feeling the soles of her feet against the carpet, then her buttocks against the seat and her spine against the back of the chair. Gradually, she surveys her body for tightness. She notices a tense feeling at the base of her neck, deliberately intensifies it by tightening the muscles for a few seconds, then allows them to relax while she exhales deliberately. She continues the exercise.

After a few minutes, she opens her eyes, noticing that the area around her looks brighter and sharper. She rises from her chair, smiles, takes a deep breath, stretches, and heads for the conference room. She is looking forward to the coming meeting.

Notes:
The G and Five C's

Get grounded. Be clear, calm, and ready.
- Feel your feet on the floor, buttocks on the chair.
- Breathe!
- Take care of business.

Make contact.
- Look.
- Say hello.
- Hear and show that you heard.

Specify the contract. Ask:
- What do you want to see happen?
- What does the other person want to see happen?
- Are these wants reasonable for the time available?

Be concrete.
- Ask who, what, where, when, and how (not why).
- Make statements that are sharp, simple, and specific.

Check. Take time out for a measurement. Ask:
- How are we doing on our joint objective?
- How are we doing at working together?

Close well. Good endings make good beginnings.
- Wrap it up.
- Specify who does what by when.
- Specify what doesn't get done.

-

CHAPTER THREE

What's on Top Comes First

Henry, a senior vice president I knew, used to say, "When I was just starting out, I had this ambition to become a top executive. There I would be, the captain of the ship, plotting the course, holding the huge wheel in my hands, steering first this way, and then that way. Now I am a top executive, and here I stand with the wheel in my hands. The only trouble is, it doesn't seem to be connected to anything."

As Henry wryly noticed, just plotting the course and turning the wheel doesn't always work. There's a lot of distracting activity going on down there in the engine room. Managing is more of a sport, it turns out, than a drill in steering and control, and as in most sports, a key requirement is good reflexes.

This chapter is intended to help you to sharpen your personal skills in thinking about and sensing your self, your environment, and your possibilities for action. Management work, in particular, presents the kinds of challenges that call for these skills, but while this chapter concentrates on managers almost all the points it makes apply to nonmanagers as well. If you are not a manager, this chapter will also help you to see better what life is like for your boss.

A seldom talked about reality of management work is that no matter how hard you try to plan it, *60 to 99 percent of managing is a matter of reacting.* So, if you're going to spend the majority of your time reacting, you need to develop good management reflexes. This development is mostly a matter of getting a steady footing (what quarterbacks call "planting yourself"), broadening your view of the field (using peripheral vision), and sharpening your awareness of what's happening both outside and inside you, so that you can pick your target (receiver) and execute your intention (throw the pass).

Management Realities

Classically, the purpose of management work has been to bring orderliness and dependability to organizational activities, but the actualities of management work in our times are different:

- Goals are multiple, unclear, and ever changing.

- Managers are continually busy with brief, disorderly, and impromptu activities. The day is mostly rush, not reflection, and that pattern of activity gets to be exciting, exhausting, and habit forming.

- Often, long-range planning in organizations is more a matter of going through the motions than producing a plan. The plan frequently has little to do with what will really happen because technology and markets change too fast.

- Some things cannot be comfortably delegated downward, especially key contacts and the things a manager's boss is most interested in. (If you don't know what's going on in detail, or if something goes sour, it's your fault, not the fault of the person to whom you delegated.)

- Managers never get all the authority they think they ought to have, no matter how high they are promoted, and eventually, that lack of authority becomes the prevailing excuse for things that go wrong.

- Any number of people and conditions above, below, and lateral to a manager can screw up the manager's projects, no matter how logical and sensible the projects are, and they frequently do.

- Decision making, like the weather, is always changing. Everybody talks about the need for its improvement, but it just keeps going its own way.

- No management method or approach works well indefinitely. Yet it's very difficult to change methods. Even when the consequences of not changing seem dire, people always seem to think something unforeseen will turn up and save them. (And sometimes it does.)

- A manager who acts fast is called a knee-jerker. A manager who doesn't act fast is called a dinosaur.

- Just because a manager has the title and the corner office (or the one with the window) doesn't mean that everyone will do what the manager wants them to.

- Almost nothing in organizations ever gets done finally and for sure (except going out of business).

- Good intentions hardly ever stand up against daily urgency and bad habits, especially when, like the lumberjack, you are just too busy chopping down trees to stop and sharpen your axe.

Sharpening Your Management Reflexes

If you are willing to entertain the heretical notion that, for most of a manager's day, planned management is an oxymoron, and probably wouldn't work well even if it could be done, then you are ready for the notion that one of the more important things a manager can learn is to be a skilled reactor. As a manager, you have to learn to deal with what's on top of the list of daily demands.

Let me make it clear that I'm talking about what you do *most* of the time. If reacting is *all* you do—if you run so hard that you are too busy to notice that you haven't been going anywhere—your days will never get any better. Worse yet, you get used to the rush of activity—until one day the gears jam, and suddenly, you're looking up from a supine position, shaking your head and asking what happened. (In addition to reacting well, you need to get off the treadmill from time to time to do some quiet pondering and to see if you are still rolling in the right direction. In later chapters, I will focus on how you step off the treadmill.)

Interestingly, most people have a natural inclination to be reactors. The problem is that many of us aren't very skillful at it. We run into three main difficulties:

- *We tend to get distracted easily*, like the batter who takes his eye off the ball.
- *Our range of response is too confined by past habits*, like the tennis player who sticks to baseline tennis in a net-game era.

64

- *We don't perceive clearly what we are reacting to*, like a boxer who ducks a left-hook feint and gets caught by a right uppercut.

Here are specific instances of the ways you and I dull our abilities to react.

Being Out of Touch

Jake Collins interrupted his boss. "My division can handle the Carter product. We've handled tough accounts before. It's simply a matter of drawing a line in the sand and telling them that's as far as we go."

George Adamson grimaced. George was Jake's boss, and he very seldom showed emotion. But this time Jake saw him definitely grimace, and Jake mentally kicked himself. He had done it again, let his mouth run away from his good sense. As he glanced quickly around the conference table he could see that his peers weren't terribly thrilled either. Jane Romano actually rolled her eyes at the ceiling.

"I'm sure," she said, "that your division would blast straight ahead and take no prisoners. But I don't think that's the point, Jake. We do have a quality problem with the product, and even if we could get Carter to agree on a settlement, we'd still have the problem with other customers."

Jake's mind hardened. "Carter doesn't have a leg to stand on. The contract doesn't specify a quality standard other than yield performance. We need to remind them about that." Jake reacted as he usually did when challenged; he counterattacked.

He had worked for Globaltech for seven years and had done well. He knew that people thought of him as a hard-charging,

65

super-assertive manager, and he liked that. It had probably been a big contributor to his promotion to division manager, but in this job, it was killing him. He could feel himself losing points with both his boss and his peers. The nervous energy just seemed to rush through him and out his mouth, which seemed to have just one mode—forward at top speed. It wasn't that he was trying to take over the meeting. That wasn't his objective. Hell, he didn't have an objective, and still everything seemed to be coming out wrong.

Ron Lefkowitz, the quality analyst, asked, "Has anybody done any estimating of the time we need to fix the quality problem?"

Jane said, "Probably three to five months."

Someone else at the table said that seemed reasonable, and someone else agreed. But by that time, Jake's mind had wandered away. He knew he had lost their attention, and the discussion no longer claimed his. His mind began a chain of wondering: Where had he gone wrong? Was he missing a point that everyone else in the room was seeing? Had he offended George? Had he completely lost his credibility with his peers? What effect would that have on his ability to run his division? What would it mean to his career? The chain of thoughts wheeled around inside his head for the remainder of the meeting and the rest of the day as well.

Speeding to Obscure Destinations

Your reactions are often limited when you don't know what you want or where you want to go, so you do what you did last time and the time before that.

Consider the customer support manager who once achieved

recognition and congratulations for having increased her organization's productivity level, but two years later, she seems to be hearing nothing but complaints. Her boss, the general manager, complains about the number of customers who call him directly to get service expedited. Her peers complain that few of the technicians in her department seem to understand the technology of the newer products. The organization's customers (those who aren't calling the boss) complain that service technicians have to keep coming back to fix what they have supposedly already fixed. The customer support manager's response is to increase the technicians' call quotas and to work much harder at her old strategy, at exhorting the technicians to work faster. In this situation, though, her old strategy was apparently inappropriate. It wasn't working. The problem wasn't resolved until her boss intervened and moved technical services out of her department.

The No-Change Airport

People also dull their ability to react by desensitizing themselves. In organizations, desensitization often results from boredom with the job. It also happens when a person is emotionally beaten-up so badly or so often by a boss or peers that it becomes just too painful to stay fully involved in the action. The person cuts off feelings of sadness or frustration and goes onto automatic pilot. You can see people doing that in meetings; they are the ones who seem only 10 percent present. Just one of the problems of working on automatic pilot is that it always takes you to the "no-change airport," where all flights start again for the same destination.

Riding the Mental Monorail

The mental monorail is yet another obstacle to perception. Riding this monorail, you stop at no stations for others' ideas to get on your train, or for any of your own ideas to get off. Monorail-mindedness frequently arises when you are so invested in your own particular model of the situation that you miss what other people are saying and doing. Have you ever watched two people in a meeting doing a dialogue of the deaf, being so rabid about the points they have to make that they talk right past each other as though they were discussing two different topics? If you watch closely, you will notice that they seldom look at one another as they talk, except when they get into a yelling match. When that happens, at last they are finally on the same topic.

Mind Delving

Fuzzing over perceptive abilities by second-guessing is also common. You imagine what is going on in other people's minds. You guess or fantasize about the other person's plans or plots, or get hooked into continually wondering what kind of impression you are making. The poet Robert Burns called it a gift "to see ourselves as others see us." The fact is, though, that others generally see you in a number of different ways that depend as much on their own needs and biases as on your actual behavior. If you get too preoccupied with how others are judging you, it will throw you off your stride.

This isn't to say that information about what particular people like and don't like about *specific* ways you operate is irrelevant. This information can be very useful for improving your effectiveness, but it needs to be collected and organized in a functional way, not as random phantom impressions. (Later, I will make some suggestions about how to gather such information.)

Of course, all of us from time to time get involved in these mind games. They can be fun and useful on occasion. But used habitually, they produce confusion and drain away the power and influence we get from having clear targets and unambiguous intentions.

Getting Grounded

If you want to be a skilled reactor you need good reflexes. The grounding process I described earlier form the base on which good reflexes are built. When you're not grounded you feel unsure, nervous, easily distracted. You may be confused and retreat, or you may overreact. Your self-boundaries are blurred, and you may be overly concerned with what you imagine others are thinking (or you may set a wall between you and others and try to disregard them totally). You may find yourself preoccupied with the past or the future, without a sound base in the present.

As the grounding exercise I introduced shows, getting grounded is simple, though not necessarily easy. There are a number of ways to think about grounding. Trees are grounded. They have roots into the earth that support them against the gusts and storms that buffet them. Good electrical systems are also grounded. Short circuits and sudden surges don't knock them out; instead, excess and dysfunctional current is quickly carried off without harm into the ground.

For individuals, grounding can be summarized as a state of

self-contained stability. You, the self-contained individual, are altogether "present" and ready for action. When you are grounded, your mind is clear and your body and emotions are alert. Your attention and awareness are available for you to focus wherever you choose, and you are ready to respond to whatever comes up, even when it's not routine.

Good grounding is the foundation of your capacity to operate as an individual. It enables you to focus on and influence what's important in your environment, to let go of distractions. Taking the time to get grounded helps you to avoid dysfunctional ego trips when things go well and to endure the knocks and burdens when they don't. Grounding is the stable base from which you, as an individual, can react to the daily activities and challenges of your job. It is also the base from which you select your personal options and mobilize to achieve them.

Broadening Awareness: Tuning In to Possibilities

Total reliance on standard procedures, on policies, and especially on "the data" and its analysis can be compelling. Standard procedures, after all, are tried and true and statistics are objective and rational. Procedures and statistics promise to take the uncertainties and guess work out of decisions, but they don't. Having your attention buried either in past conventions or the data can prevent you from seeing what's changing in your environment. A classic example was the failure of U.S. auto executives to anticipate or respond to the trend away from big, gas-guzzling cars, and to realize the threat from foreign competition.

In contrast, other companies have quickly noticed or even

70

anticipated change, broken with continuity, and made radical choices. Print media executives who successfully diversified into electronic media, contact lens manufacturers who gambled on disposable lenses and won, and scores of computer hardware and software developers became aware enough to leave well-traveled paths in favor of new ones.

It probably won't come as a surprise, then, that definitive, rational answers to many organizational issues are few and infrequent. In fact, definitive, rational answers can be Mr. Spock–logical and still off target. In the late seventies, General Motors developed a strategy to gain market share by out-spending the other two major U.S. car manufacturers in developing fuel-efficient cars. GM had vastly more resources than its competitors, so the plan was definitive and eminently rational. It didn't work. The Japanese auto manufacturers captured the market share GM had aimed for. GM's awareness was insufficient. They hadn't even taken the Japanese seriously.

Internal Awareness Signals: The I-Senses

An old organizational adage says, "The smaller and easier the problem, the more time it is likely to get in the staff meeting." Concentrating on the small, easy problems is comfortable. Dealing with the big, poorly defined ones is not. What's on top of a manager's list is often not well defined or comfortable to deal with. In making guesses, estimating, and playing hunches, you have to take risks. You have to become aware of and tune into your own internal resources. Your awareness must focus both on the external signals that tell you what's happening in your environment, and on your internal signals that help you know what you want to do about it.

71

You and I come equipped with **intuition, insight,** and **inspiration,** as well as our other marvelous and subtle sensing instruments. What are these three I-senses?

Intuition is a quick and spontaneous knowledge of what's required. It is not based on careful analysis. You know that Thursday is the right day to call on the customer just because you know it.

Insight is the power to see beyond surface messages and data into the inner nature of an opportunity, issue, or problem. You cut through symptoms to the cause. For example, your insight might tell you that the reason the development engineers haven't solved their problem isn't because they haven't had enough time to work it out with computer models; it's because they haven't gone into the lab and worked with the actual material.

Inspiration is that inexplicable power that actuates and mobilizes your energy and carries you into new territories of thought and feeling. Charismatic leaders can inspire you, but so can your own spirit.

Though I know of no definitive study on the matter, my hunch is that just about every individual, including those who would be most uncomfortable admitting it, has used these senses early in his or her life. For a variety of reasons, some people (sometimes unintentionally) learn to shut down these senses. Either they don't believe the senses are valid, or they have been taught to think that these senses are irrational or unscientific and therefore unacceptable. The good news is that if you have learned to shut your I-senses down and you later change your mind you can also learn to turn them on again.

Some of you are not going to be immediately tempted to

turn on your I-senses. You may worry that turning them on will make your life more hectic or even run it out of control. But increasing your spectrum of awareness doesn't mean that you are no longer in charge of your decisions. It just means that you increase your options for action. It can also make your work more satisfying.

Relevant Emotional Awareness

Another part of the awareness spectrum that not many people in organizations talk about much anymore is emotional awareness. Spending time on the emotional aspects of organization life has been frowned upon since the late seventies. It's too "touchy-feely."

The negative reaction is understandable. Like any number of other popular trends, the sensitivity movement was driven too fast by too many advocates who were insufficiently aware of the basic requirements of business environments. Organizations charged with achieving discrete results on limited schedules didn't have time for the often fascinating yet often tangential detours devoted to wandering down the lanes of personal sensibilities.

But that reaction does not mean that feelings and relationships are of no importance in organizations. Understanding who in a department is for or against whom, who bears grudges, who prizes loyalty above all other qualities, who gets mad when asked about his golf scores, and so on is important. Recognizing what turns people on or sets them off is a critical element in your awareness of your external environment. If you ignore that element, no matter how good your rational skills, you're playing with half a deck.

73

People don't leave their emotions at home. Individuals in organizations have many feelings about each other, and sometimes these feelings get in the way of business. Effective people keep track of what needs doing, and they are also aware of the emotional factors that can facilitate or hinder their aims.

Tuning out your emotional awareness can be dysfunctional for both you and your organization. If you are tuned out, you may not recognize or express either affection or irritation, appreciation or a sense of urgency. The tuned-out person who is unaware of dissatisfaction or resentment about a subordinate's job performance cannot articulate the problem, does not bring it to the subordinate's attention, and gets no corrective action. The prevalence of tuned-out managers may help to explain why so many managers avoid counseling and appraisal sessions with their subordinates and why so many of the sessions that are held are of poor quality.

Probably what is most dysfunctional when people outlaw their emotional awareness is that they never deal with their own feelings. So emotions such as irritation or anger continue as unfinished business. Tuned-out managers may find indirect ways of exercising resentments, perhaps by treating subordinates coolly, withholding support, or subtly snubbing them. But even subtle negative expression will probably affect the subordinate, who will react first with confusion and subsequently with her own version of resistance or resentment. So a circular process of resentment and counter-resentment continues to widen the gap between those involved. And the employee is denied an opportunity to improve her job performance, and her future career suffers.

Being aware of your feelings does not mean you have to act them out (nor that you are prohibited from doing so). Your action should depend on what makes sense to you.

74

The awareness workout exercise that follows will give you some basic awareness practice. It can loosen up your I-sense "muscles" if your habit has been to hold your thinking to a conventional rational/logical framework. The exercise calls for you and the others with whom you participate to take a step or two beyond your usual ways of interacting in order to get in touch with your own intuition, insight, and inspiration. What comes out, at least ĩn the early stages of the exercise, will probably not be logical. Nevertheless, it may make a great deal of sense. The awareness exercise seems to produce a different kind of communication than the one we are used to. But don't try for too much too early. Like any other basic workout, the exercise usually takes a while before it produces noticeable improvement and you begin to carry your new awareness with you naturally wherever you go.

Good feelings often accompany the awareness exercise, but those feelings are only part of the picture. The main point of the exercise is to practice temporarily setting aside your need to be active. Instead, you are practicing *allowing*. Like a big dish antenna, you have opened up your receivers to a broader range of frequencies. As you practice this or other exercises in this book, it can be helpful to work and share discoveries with a few friends or co-workers who are also interested in processes of self-discovery.

Exercise: An Awareness Workout

It's a good idea to try this exercise the first time or two with people that you know fairly well (your spouse or friends). You can do it with two people but starting with three or four is easier.

1. Sit facing each other in a comfortable position. *Take a moment to get grounded.*

2. Speaking in rotation, each person makes a statement of awareness, beginning with the words, "Right now, I am aware of . . ." The person reports whatever comes into his or her *immediate* awareness. It is important to report awareness as it happens, rather than rehearse an answer. Here is a sample dialogue:

   MR. A: "Right now, I am aware of your red tie."

   MS. B: "Right now, I am aware of my back against the chair."

   MR. A: "Right now, I am aware of thinking. (When you find yourself thinking about something specific, it's not necessary, or even desirable, to report the subject matter. Merely report that you are thinking; then let go of the thought and see what comes into your awareness next.)"

   MS. B: "Right now, I am aware of feeling calmer."

   MR. A: "Right now, I am aware of the sun shining through the window."

At any point in a round, when something comes into awareness that you do not want to share, feel free to say "pass."

3. Continue around the circle. Don't try to build rational conversations or send messages to one another; let the

awareness come spontaneously. ("Don't just do something, stand there!") Concentrate on your senses—what you see, hear, feel, and so on. If you become bored, uncomfortable, or confused, just report that as well, and wait it out. Those things, too, will pass, and you may be pleasantly surprised at what's on the other side.

4. After five to ten minutes, pause, and in a *brief* (five minutes or less) discussion, help each other recognize where and how each person tends to focus most of his or her attention. Is the person usually thinking, seeing, hearing, or sensing in some particular way? Don't analyze, just comment.

5. Next, try the exercise again (perhaps with another partner, if one is available), focusing on one or two senses that you have up to now mostly neglected. Do not strain to change the senses you use, but allow an easy shift of attention to occur. And remember, don't try to learn anything; just do it!

6. End the exercise by talking about your experiences *briefly*.

Now imagine yourself sitting at your next staff meeting. Your usual pattern at those meetings may be to be a listener and planner, an activist spring-loaded to make a point, or a day-dreamer who catches every third or fourth sentence, but for the next five or ten minutes, you are not going to do any of those things. Instead, you are going to get grounded and practice awareness. At a slow pace, you are going to subvocalize the words, "Right now I am aware of ..." And, without much analysis, you are going to learn a good deal about the people in the room (including yourself) and the ways they handle issues and interact.

Working Is

Working is a way
Of putting the way you are
Together with the things you need to do
In a way that satisfies you and other people.

Working is a way
Of earning your daily bread
And, if you're talented, meals in good restaurants
And of filling in your holes (or wholes) as you go along.

Working is a way
Of cooperating with others,
Competing against others, and winning
And losing, and learning to tough it out.

Notes:
What's on Top Comes First

- Most (not all) of management work is a matter of responding to day-to-day dilemmas. A good manager has to be a good reactor. To become a good reactor, sharpen your management reflexes.

- Clear targets and unambiguous intentions are the foundations of power. Broad-spectrum awareness of both the signals from your environment and your own internal signals is key to picking appropriate targets and mobilizing your will.

- The I-senses—intuition, insight, and inspiration—come as standard equipment on each human being. You choose whether or not to tune them in. If you want well-developed I-senses, practice awareness.

- When you are in good contact with your own internal signals and know what you want and where you want to go, you are more likely to make good contact with other people and the real issues that need to be resolved. Abstracting your case and diluting your message undermines your impact.

-

CHAPTER FOUR

Closing the Circle

THIS CHAPTER is about *finishing*—completing, winding up, and wrapping up—things that many people find hard to do.

Wanderers

FRANK LAXALT has to get his staff to take on more responsibility and more work. It has been a down year for Globaltech and an even tougher one for the Network Services Division, where Frank manages one of the departments. Network Services has had six losing quarters in a row. Operating budgets have been tightened to the choke point, especially among staff departments like Frank's. His staffing proposals have been turned down, and worse yet, he has been asked not to fill an existing opening.

Frank enters his conference room, but the buzz of conversation continues. He sits down and calls for the group's attention, which turns to him slowly. He begins by saying, "As we discussed last meeting, it's been decided that we can't replace the customer service rep vacancy in Mary Schwarz's area. We have to adjust our operations to cover the same amount of work with the people we have."

"Why us again?" the Northwest area supervisor asks. "The billing department got their replacement."

"They got their requisition in just under the wire," says Frank, sadly. He knows this is not going to be an easy hour.

"We could have put ours in earlier, if we had moved faster," says Northwest, glowering slightly at Mary, who is the South Central area supervisor.

"One could say it is a poor way to run a company," says the Atlantic states supervisor. "It's arbitrary."

But the Southwest supervisor has another idea. "There might be more to it than arbitrariness. Some say that Linda Germain has special influence with Sid Lowry."

Frank says, "Well, whether she does or not, don't you think we ought to work on solving *our* problem?"

"Right," agrees Southwest. "The open job is in Mary's operation. What if each of us takes on a share of her extra work? That seems fair, doesn't it?"

"That solution," replies Northwest, "is based on the assumption that the workload is evenly distributed now."

"How can one really get an exact measurement on workload," someone else says. "One can only approximate."

"Not necessarily," replies Northwest. "There are measurements that are being used now in the finance department on work effectiveness for administrative jobs."

"How can anyone compare finance jobs to our jobs?"

Frank has begun to dart quick glances toward the clock. The meeting is only scheduled for an hour. "Don't you think we should get back to Southwest's proposal about distributing the work?" he asks them.

"What if we each send one person for two hours each day over into Mary's department to work at the customer service desk? That would save time and effort, wouldn't it?" asks Northwest. This suggestion brings out a tumble of comments.

"We would have to make up schedules."

"Would we be sending the same person every time, or could we mix them?"

"It ought to be the same for the sake of consistency."

"Oh, come on, how much consistency do you need on a customer service desk? There's not much to the job."

"There's a lot more to it than some people think."

"It's an important job," Frank agrees with the last speaker, passionately. He is proud of having talked the evaluation committee into upgrading the job earlier in the year. "The job evaluation committee rated it a sixteen."

"But that was based on customer service in Atlantic states, and we were getting a lot of new business," says the Atlantic states supervisor. "South Central is pretty cut and dried."

By now Frank, too, is caught in the momentum of the chase. He launches into an explanation of his previous actions. He has forgotten himself and his department's troublesome problem, and he will not remember it again until seven minutes to the hour. Then, he will tell himself it is too late; perhaps he will cover the problem in the next meeting.

The Never-Closing Circle

Frank's and his group's inability to reach a conclusion, not just on the urgent matter of how to handle the extra work but even on the tangential subjects they raised, is an example of a *never-closing circle*. Finishing a piece of business can be blocked by less obvious emotions too. I know of people in organizations who have personal resentments and antagonisms that are years old. No one ever talks about them but they are always there, and like sand in the machinery, they grind away and slow things down or sometimes stop them entirely.

In one national sales organization, for example, personal feuds had gone on for more than a decade and had blocked all efforts over the years to develop collaborative work between regions. I was asked to meet with the group because market conditions had made collaboration a must. After working with people to identify what this ancient unfinished business was about, I finally learned that its root was a single incident. At a company conference twelve years earlier, three sales managers from the Southern states had made arrangements with another group from the Eastern seaboard to meet after dinner. But the Southern group hadn't shown up and had left the Easterners stranded at the restaurant late at night. After that beginning, the ordinary frictions of daily business had been enough to keep the feud alive and flourishing. Of course, when they finally talked about what had happened that fateful evening, it turned out to be a huge misunderstanding about where the groups were supposed to meet.

There is a wide range of causes for unclosed circles and unfinished business. There are also methods you can use to deal with the problems, *if you want to*. The methods take effort though. You have to take on responsibilities that are not part of your job description. In fact, they may seem more appropriate to someone else's job. For example, if you had been a participant in Frank Laxalt's meeting and you had decided to resolve the problem of unfinished business, you would have had to take personal responsibility for the meeting, at least temporarily. To do that would have required delicacy, skill, and some willingness to risk yourself.

Why do it? Good question. Some people wouldn't in a hundred years, and they live peaceful organizational lives. People who take on responsibility for closing circles do so because they acquire a personal drive for getting things done. They savor the satisfaction they get from accomplishing a task, and they look forward to seeing what the next task in line will look like. In an era of ever quickening change such people are valuable.

The Drift and Drop Syndrome

Taking responsibility for closing the circle isn't your only alternative. You could also insist that it's the boss's job and if she doesn't do it, that's her problem. You can wait for somebody else in the group to close the circle. Or you can watch as the *drift and drop syndrome* sets in. Issues drift whichever way the current takes them until time runs out, and then they drop into whatever resolution they are nearest at the moment (sometimes that's oblivion).

Remember Frank Laxalt and his group? In their next staff meeting, when Frank again raised the issue of what to do about the loss of a departmental position, the group continued to float away. No one ever asked whether a position from another unit ought to be transferred, nor did they get much further in developing a schedule to provide part-time help to Mary's unit. Over the months, the unit's open slot continued unfilled, and complaints from customers kept increasing.

Why Things Don't Get Finished and What You Can Do About It

Attitudes and language are key to closing circles. How people feel about their jobs, their organization, and themselves, and what kind of behavior is expected of them, largely determines their willingness to take on responsibility for closing the circle. The kind of language they use in their discussions largely determines their ability to move the circle-closing process forward.

These are the frequent reasons why people avoid taking charge of finishing business:

- *Inertia*. That's the way it's (not) done around here.
- *Apprehension*. Why stick my neck out?
- *Uncertainty*. I don't know what they or I want out of this.
- *Pessimism*. Whatever I do won't make much difference anyway.
- *Perplexity*. This decision is a tough one to take on.

The two exercises given here address these typical impediments. The exercises are for use by both work groups and individuals, and they focus on what you can do to deal with your own obstacles and restimulate your circle-closing energy.

The first exercise, Hopes and Concerns, can be used in both small- and large-group meetings. Meetings are often sluggish because participants don't know the meetings' purposes or what other participants want. Or participants suspect hidden agendas, behind the scenes motives, and pitfalls that no one talks about.

Sometimes the person who called the meeting can sense from the start that things don't feel quite right, but he or she doesn't know what's wrong or what to do about it. The Hopes and Concerns exercise can help significantly by providing an up-to-date picture of participants' emotional perspectives as well as subject matter interests. In addition, the catharsis of expressing their concerns often helps individuals move on from attitudes of frustration or despair to greater energy and commitment.

Exercise:
Hopes and Concerns

When meeting participants are familiar with the grounding and contact processes, it's good for everyone involved to go through those exercises first. Then proceed through the following steps:

1. When the group has settled down, the person who called the meeting (or the person who suggests the exercise) asks each participant to take a minute and write down the one or two things that he or she would most like to get out of this session, and the one or two things that would be the worst that could happen if the meeting went badly from the participant's point of view. The emphasis is on the individual participants' thoughts. You are not asking people to report what would be best or worst for the total organization or the other people in the group. Participants are then asked to pass their anonymous notes up front to be read out loud by a volunteer. No one is required to report anything he or she doesn't want to.

2. The volunteer lists on a blackboard or flip chart the major themes among both the hopes and concerns—for example: "Hope we get this problem settled before we leave."

"Concerned this meeting will turn into a dog and pony show."

3. The group then devotes a limited time to discussing how it can maximize the possibilities for realizing the hopes and addressing the concerns. (Don't deny or ignore the concerns.) The leader of the exercise should set up some mechanisms to monitor the meeting's progress—a time-keeper or a subject matter monitor, for example. But mostly, the leader should encourage all participants to take responsibility for getting their hopes to happen. The leader should be concrete and specific. If participants are concerned that "this meeting will be as ineffective as the last one," find out how the last one was ineffective and what they believe can be done to make it better. Ignoring the problems won't make them go away. Teams can turn around and go forward with a new sense of purpose after they've had a chance to voice and explore their hopes and complaints, and either hear clear explanations or develop a revised way of working together.

4. During the meeting itself, participants should periodically refer back to the posted lists, check how well they're doing, and adjust the meeting process accordingly. In the closing moments of the meeting, the leader asks people to take one more look at their own particular items on the lists and to indicate briefly how well they think they've done.

The second exercise, If I Were King, is, among other things, a good optimism booster and energy enhancer. You can use it all by yourself, or even better, with one or two co-workers. (Of course, both men and women can be "kings" in this game.)

Exercise:
If I Were King

1. Congratulations, you just got a big promotion. You are now king of your organization. As king, you now hold absolute sovereignty. Write down quickly, spontaneously, and explicitly a list of what you want to do.

2. When you have finished the list, select one or two items that you want to start with. What's keeping you from making them happen? (If you're working with a few others, talk about it. If alone, make some notes.) Consider these points:

   • Are the negative reactions you anticipate from others realistic, or do your fears seem imaginary when you examine them concretely?
   • Can some of your ideas be made acceptable with relatively slight modification?
   • Is the idea important enough that it might be worthwhile to put it into effect, even if it has to be done over the objections of some others?

3. Set your lists and thoughts aside for a day or two, then go back and see what you want to do next, your majesty.

Variations
A variation of the exercise can be used in a fun spirit in a team when team members have sound, open relationships.

1. Each team member develops and presents to the whole group a short list of what that person and his or her organization would do differently if he or she was king and had no concerns about the reactions of bosses or peers. The list can also include the king's "demands" on everybody else in the group.

2. After presentations have been made, take a break, then have the group come back and look at the lists more seriously. What do people suggest as real possibilities? Can some modifications be made to render some apparently outlandish ideas practicable?

Several years ago, I used this exercise with a person who had just been appointed to head a large organization. In his view, his promotion produced some serious problems. Since he had been selected from among a group of peers, several of whom thought they were qualified for the job, he felt that he needed to be very careful not to antagonize or upset any of those who now reported to him. He knew that his future success depended on their support and effective performance. It became clear that this intelligent and highly competent person was restricting himself almost to the point of paralysis out of his concern for the reactions of those who now reported to him. He scarcely allowed himself to think of the changes he wanted to make in the organization. It was to relieve some of the heaviness of this situation that I suggested to him that he play If I Were King.

Within twenty minutes, he had a list of eighteen items he wanted to initiate or change in the organization. He then reviewed the list, and with an uncharacteristic roar of enthusiasm, immediately determined that he could begin work on ten of the items without delay. For four others, he decided he would first need to do some preliminary groundwork, but the items could be carried out. He decided to abandon the remaining four.

When people cut off personal creativity and force by anticipating resistance, potential resentment, or other forms of catastrophe, If I Were King is worth a try. A point to remember in this exercise is that it's better to start with a high expectation and modify it by working your way back to realism than to start with a low expectation and modify it by inching forward. The extravagant approach is stimulating, and it opens up brand-new possibilities, rather than just minor variations of old ones.

Notes:
Closing the Circle

- Closing the circle means completing your business. It enables you to turn your attention fully to what's next. When you do not finish old business, it can trip you up later.

- Inertia, apprehension, uncertainty, pessimism, and perplexity are attitudes that obscure and obstruct your opportunities. These attitudes are often the products of undefined fantasies. Clear definition almost invariably changes them.

- Full awareness of your best possibilities does a better job of stimulating energy than a restricted goal inhibited by old "practicalities." Begin by thinking big.

-

CHAPTER FIVE

Handling Predicaments

AT TIMES, the main obstacle to closing the circle is the difficulty of the issue. In these predicaments, the pros and cons seem just too closely balanced for comfort. You feel like Hamlet—"To be or not to be, that is the question." There are analytical techniques for studying the substance of predicaments. For example, Force-field Analysis is a problem-solving tool that helps you to array and examine the positives and negatives in a situation and think about ways to enhance the former and minimize the latter. Such analytical approaches can be helpful, but sometimes they don't address the nonanalytical elements of the predicament. You need to tap into your I-senses of intuition, insight, and inspiration (see Chapter Three), plus your feelings and your energy, to get at the nonanalytical parts of the total answer. The *polarization* process and exercise described in this chapter can help you answer certain hard questions, especially those where people are affected and doing the right thing is important to you.

The Polarization Process

The harder you push yourself, the harder yourself is likely to push back. And that can make you quite tired.

93

Fritz Perls, the Gestalt theorist I mentioned in the introduction, pointed out that each of us has within us a *topdog* and an *underdog*. As Joen Fagan and Irma Lee Shepherd describe Perls's theory, in *Gestalt Therapy Now* (1970), topdog is that part of ourselves that tells us what's "proper" and appropriate for our behavior, and even for our thoughts. Most topdog positions are derived from "shouldisms" that we learned from parents, bosses, and other authority figures. Topdog is the persistent voice inside you that says you *should* keep your opinions and suggestions about the department managers' meetings to yourself, even though the meetings never seem to go anywhere. It also tells you that it's wrong for you to keep postponing that counseling session with Fred, your subordinate. Topdog can be felt as conscience or goad, and its thrust can be, and has been for most of us, very useful in influencing our actions. Problems arise, though, when the topdog's demands are met by the underdog's resistance.

Our underdog is a subtle yet powerful counterforce to our topdog's driving force. The underdog may resist in a number of ways. It may reply to the topdog's demands, "I want to do what you say, but I'm not able," or, "I'd like to, and I'll do it tomorrow" (although, of course, the underdog doesn't do it tomorrow either). Underdog is also good at excuses—for example, "Don't you know how busy I am?" or, "But, if I do that then something bad might happen," and so on.

Many of the unresolved, nagging issues that individuals experience are the consequences of a stalemate between their topdogs and underdogs. The signs of this stalemate are indecision, confusion, and frustration.

Fritz Perls calculated that, in the contest between topdog

and underdog, underdog usually wins, especially in the long run. But the winning or losing is not as important as the energy, frustration, and guilt feelings that so frequently accompany this internal battle of ambivalence. What is most troubling to us is not that we go out fishing on the weekend rather than finishing the report that's due Monday, but that we spend half our time feeling guilty about not being at home working on the report.

What can you do about these polarities? The most important step is to work toward *clarity and completion*, to move the battleground from the inside of your head to a place where each side of the argument can be clearly drawn and the arguments fully detailed and the circle closed. At best, when you fully explore your polarities, the extremes of your position, you may find a new integration. *Integration* is not a compromise position, somewhere between the extremes. You don't usually reach it by a neat, balanced process. Integration *happens* when it is ready to. It appears in the form of a fresh, creative, surprising answer that wasn't available to you before.

The following exercise, Working Your Polarities, will help you experience your polarities and, eventually, integration.

Exercise:
Working Your Polarities

1. Think of a problem in which you are currently having some difficulty making a decision because of ambivalent feelings. Write the problem down in a few sentences— for example, Should I give Fred a raise at his next performance review or skip his increase this time?

2. Write a dialogue of the argument you are having with yourself about this question. Let the dialogue be

spontaneous; don't censor yourself or worry about being silly or unreasonable. Only you will see your notes. Also, don't worry about which arguer is topdog and which is underdog. You may not know that until the whole dialogue has been completed. This is how part of a dialogue might look:

ME 1: You ought not give Fred the raise because his performance hasn't been very good this year.

ME 2: Well, Fred has been trying hard; it's just that he has been having a lot of trouble.

ME 1: You're not supposed to pay people more money for trying hard, you're supposed to pay for results.

ME 2: There are a lot of people in other departments in this organization who aren't doing any better than Fred but who will probably get a raise this year. I might get a reputation as a hard-nosed manager.

ME 1: That's not the point, and you know it. If you give him the raise, you will have less budget for your better performers, and if you don't get the message across to Fred that he is in serious trouble, he won't change.

3. Continue writing the dialogue until you have either come to a conclusion or come to an impasse—that is, you feel that there is nothing more you are willing to say to yourself in either role. Put your dialogue aside for a while, maybe overnight, and do something else.

4. When you are ready, re-read your dialogue. To the extent you're able, read it with a fresh perspective, as though it

had been written by someone else. As you read, underline those words and phrases that particularly catch your attention or seem important to you. See if you have come closer to reaching a decision and/or picked up new insights.

Variation

Another way of doing this exercise is to find a place that's quiet and private. Set up two chairs facing one another and speak the dialogue out loud, as spontaneously as you can, moving from chair to chair as the speaker changes. It is also helpful to record the exercise so you can listen to yourself afterward. As you listen, see if you can recognize in which chair you are most energetic, and in which chair your voice is strongest and your points made most decisively.

After you have concluded your own topdog-underdog dialogue, you can learn still more about your own attitudes and their relevance by using the dialogue technique (either in writing or speaking) for an imaginary conversation between yourself and Fred. Say what you would say to him if you decided to hold the discussion and then what you believe he would answer. Don't be too concerned about accurately predicting what Fred would *really* say. There is no way of knowing that. What you are doing is getting a clearer picture of where *you* stand, both with yourself and with your imaginings of what goes on in Fred's mind and feelings. If, after you've finished the dialogue, you have some new ideas and you decide to talk to Fred in person, do not get hung up in trying to duplicate the imaginary dialogue in the real conversation. Deal with Fred in a totally fresh way. Start by making contact.

When I was young, people used to say that those who talked to themselves weren't necessarily crazy—unless they answered back. But in recent years, a number of psychologists have concluded that talking to yourself through silent, repetitive thoughts can indeed make you crazy by its futility. When you bring your dialogue out into the open, though, and lend it the substance of your voice or pen, you may well have started on the right track to personal clarity, a healthier outlook, and closing some circles.

Language That Tarries, Language That Moves

Meandering discussion is not always bad. As a product of intention rather than accident, it can encourage free expression. It may even release a flow of creativity. But it is not conducive to sharpening your focus or accomplishing a purpose. If unfinished business describes the perpetual status of most agenda items in an organization, that organization is probably on its way to trouble. Some issues do go away by themselves, others drift and drop into tolerable slots, but there will always be a few that reach out long tentacles to trip you up, no matter what your level in the organization.

Among many management groups, especially at senior levels, the response to rambling meetings has been to set tightly structured agendas. You give your report on the weekly, monthly, or quarterly results, the boss and sometimes your peers ask questions and make nice or nasty comments, then the meeting rolls on to the next victim. That process, of course, usually takes the life out of the session and brings out only the required minimum of information. (The less information, the smaller the target for potshots.)

One set of reasons for nonmoving interaction comprises the self-restricting attitudes I spoke of earlier, which are sometimes intentional and sometimes not. A second set is based on a communication style that features an inappropriate (usually unintended) preoccupation with description or prescription, the languages of abstraction. You can become immediately smarter and more influential if you only learn to notice the level of the abstraction ladder at which you and another person are communicating. And it's easy.

The abstraction ladder has three rungs: about, should, and is. The top rung is *about*. Communicating at this level, you deal with your world as a set of concepts. You concentrate on ideas, theories, and principles, and you treat these abstractions as though they were at arm's length from you. You might describe a certain situation this way:

"The hazards of storing combustible materials in proximity with sources of high ambient temperatures are currently illustrated."

The middle rung of the ladder is *should*. Here you are under the strong influences of the norms, traditions, role models, and habits that provide your rules and regulations for operating. Communicating at this level, you would describe the same situation this way:

"Now perhaps you'll believe me when I say you should store oily rags in a sealed container."

At the bottom rung, close to the ground, is *is*—the place

where movement happens. Communicating at this level, you would handle the same situation by saying,

"The place is on fire. Get a fire extinguisher!"

Each of these styles of communicating and operating has its uses. I emphasize the *is* style, however, because it is so often neglected; yet it is a powerful tool for influencing people and getting things to happen, rather than merely discussed.

About

Talking *about* can be very useful, even essential, much of the time. This book talks *about* concepts and ideas that I believe can be useful and that I want to convey to you. An employee who has a new idea of how to improve a work process needs to talk *about* his idea to others. In describing the elements of a re-organization she is considering, a manager would undoubtedly find it useful to talk *about* the intentions and benefits of the proposed new structures. Conceptualizing is, of course, also important in exploring ideas and possibilities for the future.

Talking *about* situations is less useful, and sometimes even dysfunctional, when, as in the example of Frank Laxalt's staff discussion, people continue to use anecdotes, reminiscences, and speculations to divert action, instead of dealing with a specific and immediate issue.

There are some clear clues for identifying *about* talk. The personal pronoun "I" is seldom used. Instead, words like "we," "one," or the general "you" or "the company" are substituted, thereby dissociating speakers from their own statements, and often diminishing their impact on listeners as well, since it's unclear to the listeners (and sometimes to the speakers) where the speakers stand on an issue or how important it is to them.

For example, when a manager intended to transfer an important planning function to a new department, he tried to justify the move to the department head who was losing the function by using several reasons based on organization theory, concluding that "the organization will benefit from the change and will be more effective." The department head, nevertheless, was unconvinced and dissatisfied.

Only after several days of argument and mounting feelings of frustration was the manager finally willing to take a personal position and to lay out his specific reason for wanting to make the change. He said, "I'm not satisfied with the way the function is being performed now."

At that point, he and the department head were able to begin constructive discussions. In this particular case, the clearing of the air and focus on specifics resulted in a provisional agreement to continue the planning function in its present department, contingent upon the implementation of a series of changes in the process.

Should

The principal sources of *should* are mind-models, images you carry around that describe for you the way the world is supposed to be. Models are necessary and helpful for guidance, but it's useful to remind yourself that your model is only one of a number of possible models. An inability to recognize other models is *model myopia*. Such myopia can keep you from noticing significant elements that do not fit your image but are nevertheless important.

Shoulds are usually based on norms, standards, traditions, role models, and preachments that you and I have been learning from infancy on. At best, your *shoulds* provide you with a sense of moral and ethical direction. They can also provide a guideline (for example, the scientific method) for pursuing a particular variety of truth or success. At worst, they can lock you into a counterproductive point of view. For instance, if you are stuck in the judgment that the U.S. industrial system *should* just keep doing what it has been doing, or that quality inspection *should* always be separated from the people who produce the product, or that economies of scale *should* always be the way to become efficient, or that women in business *should* be seen but not heard, you could be seriously out of touch.

Shoulds play a large part in determining management roles. Individuals' ideas of proper managerial behavior are gathered from a number of sources. Formal sets of rules may be provided by an organization, and in some companies, these rules may deal not only with work situations but also with personal conduct off the job. Sometimes the rules aren't formal, but "everybody knows" what's expected. Ideas of managerial behavior may be contained in organizational folklore or traditions of good managership. They may come from observations (frequently incomplete) of senior manager hero figures (introjections), from managerial stereotypes, or from one or more of the multitude of management training programs that have sprouted like dandelions all over the world.

Some *shoulds* can serve as sound guidelines—a manager should balance company needs and employee interests. Others can inhibit creative problem solving—each department should be responsible for dealing with its own problems. And still others can be downright dysfunctional—a manager should always maintain tight controls over all organizational activities.

At a minimum, *shoulds* are the rules of the game. At a maximum, they hold the existing order of things together. In fact, some individuals worry that if people don't hold to the *shoulds* the world will move toward chaos. Some think it's moving that way now.

The exercise Getting to Know Your Shoulds is aimed at helping you to identify and explore some of your *shoulds*. It's not intended to convince you that you *should* change. The operating premise in this book is that *useful change in human beings occurs naturally, and starts with awareness*. Few, if any, people in the world are completely open at all times. Most of us modify our behavior in a great many ways and in accordance with a variety of situations. Of course, I'm not advocating that you as an individual *should* make a new resolution to always "be yourself." If you were to make that resolution and try to live up to it, you would merely be taking on another set of *shoulds*.

Exercise:
Getting to Know Your Shoulds

1. Write a list of five important *shoulds* (or *should nots*) you have accepted for yourself as a manager (or as a subordinate, spouse, parent, son, or daughter, and so forth). Write more or less than five if you like, unless you feel you *should* write five. Be as concrete and specific as possible.

2. Try to identify the source for each item, that is, from where the *should* came to you—for example, from company policy, your boss, your early training, and so forth.

3. For each of the *shoulds* and *should nots*, note specifically
   how you imagine you would act if you were to allow
   yourself to follow your own natural inclinations instead of
   the *should* or *should not*. Would your behavior be the same
   or different?

4. Briefly, write out how you stop yourself from following your
   own natural inclinations for each of the items. For
   example, you may imagine that following your own
   inclinations would result in your disappointing such
   people as your boss or subordinates, or you may think
   people in the organization would think less of you.

5. Now, for a moment, imagine yourself in the place of the
   particular individual or individuals who would be
   disappointed by your behavior. Do your negative
   expectations stand up?

6. If it's important to you, and seems possible and practical,
   arrange a time to sit down with one or more of the people
   you have identified and discuss with them appropriate
   parts of your list (that is, how you now operate versus how
   you would like to operate) and get their reactions. (Use
   the G and five C's approach discussed in Chapter Two.) Be
   especially alert to the possibility that your expectation of
   their negative reactions may not be entirely accurate.
   They may be more willing to have you move toward the
   kind of behavior you would like for yourself than you
   originally thought. Also, be aware of the possibility of a
   reciprocal bargain with the other person. Ask if there are

ways in which he or she would like to interact with you but refrains from doing so. Look for potential new arrangements and trade-offs that can enhance both your work life and your colleagues'. Short simple sentences are especially useful in these discussions, particularly sentences that begin with a straightforward statement of what you want of the other person. And encourage him or her to express briefly and clearly what he or she wants of you. Make notes of the results of your conversations.

7. After you have completed the first six steps, take another look at your original list of *shoulds* and *should nots* and see if there are some changes that you now feel prepared to try out. Don't push yourself too hard. Start with relatively easy changes, get some experience, and then go on to further work and discussions with others on additional changes you would like to make in the ways you do certain things.

The Getting to Know Your Shoulds exercise can be used within a small team to enhance work relationships. Ask team members to join you in preparing lists of *shoulds* and invite them, if they are willing, to work out their *wants* of you in similar ways. Taking several hours or even half a day away from the office with your team on this exercise and working in an open way with each other can be a very valuable, productive means of improving satisfaction and effectiveness in your own organization.

Is

Is is where the action is.

Being in the *is* mode means being aware of, recognizing, and dealing with what is currently on top—what is happening now. You may like what's happening or not, you may approve or not. What is happening may fit your notion of what should be happening or it may not.

Dealing with what *is* means keeping your message simple and keeping yourself connected to it. For instance:

"I would like to see this team reach a conclusion about how we are going to handle this issue."

"I agree with Judy on this."

"I want to make a proposal."

"I believe that we are headed for trouble if we don't change this procedure."

Dealing with the *is* doesn't mean that you give vent to every impulse or feeling that crosses your mind or that you have to be compulsively outspoken, informing your secretary that you don't like her hairstyle, or your boss that you don't think she handled her last meeting with the board of directors very well. In fact, being compulsive about voicing your honest opinions in all circumstances is another form of shouldism.

Addressing the *is* involves using your skilled awareness to extend and sharpen your individual perception of a given situation. When a problem comes over the horizon, you don't deny its existence to yourself and everyone else. You perceive it and make a conscious choice as to whether and how to deal with it now. There is a narrow but important line between positive thinking and self-delusion. Confidence and optimism about your ability to handle a problem is one thing, blinding yourself

106

to a problem's existence is another. If the economy is in a recession and your company has been cutting back its work force, you recognize the situation, rather than deny it, and then, tuning into both your analytical abilities and your intuitive ones, you decide whether it's time to start preparing your résumé and the best places to send it.

Notes:
Handling Predicaments

- Like fear, an unconfronted barrier tends to be more threatening than one faced head-on. Even when you can't find a way through it, you can often find a way over, under, or around it.

- *About* is for consideration; *should* is for ethical guidance; *is* is for action.

-

PART TWO

STAYING CENTERED IN KEY WORK RELATIONSHIPS

THIS SECTION is about the nitty-gritty of governing your job. It talks about the need to step off the treadmill of routine for a fresh look at what you are doing and how well it is getting you what you want and where you want to go. I describe a process for entering a new job (or taking a fresh look at your current job) and a way to take stock of your opportunities and obstacles.

This section also focuses on your relations with both your boss and your subordinates. It looks at ways to manage your manager so that he or she contributes to, rather than gets in the way, of your doing your job. There are also ways to help you assess your own management style and to separate useful from useless intelligence about how your subordinates think you are performing.

CHAPTER SIX

Stepping off the Treadmill

THIS CHAPTER is about taking time for a fresh, focused look at what you are doing and how you're doing it. It can help you start a new job or start your current job anew. It begins by suggesting some personal processes for starting a new job, including gaining impressions of the people and situations you will be working with and recognizing the opportunities and obstacles they present. Most of the same approaches are applicable even if you have been in your job for a while. They will help you to refresh and sharpen your perspectives. I focus on a management job, but most of the points I make apply equally well to other jobs and roles.

Starting a New Job: Gaining Impressions

Hank said, "There are at least three wrong ways to start a new management job. You can come on like a tiger, a rabbit, or a honey bear. The tigers charge in, roar loudly or growl menacingly, and announce the way things are going to be. The rabbits are cautious and try not to make waves. In fact, sometimes they even try not to leave any tracks. Then there are the

111

honey bears, who seem to want only to be well liked. I say seem, because you can never quite be sure how much bear is still left in the honey bear until the crunch."

Pete said, "The tiger sounds like me."

They were at the Hungry Halibut, and Pete was thinking to himself that his idea of asking old Hank Bloom out to dinner was a good one. Hank Bloom had been a department manager at Globaltech longer than practically anyone remembered, and his advice was usually pretty good. Having just been promoted to his first management job, Pete figured he could use the help. The grapevine talk he had heard was that department manager jobs in this division of the company were tough.

Hank grinned, "Yes, your style, as I remember, is like the guy who comes into General Electric, and immediately begins by telling everyone the way we used to do things at IBM. Not a winning tactic."

"Well, none of the three sounds very winning. What do you suggest?"

"Stay inscrutable for a while."

"What?"

"That's right. At the start, don't go out of your way to be the strong new leader or the friendly new boss."

"Well, if I'm not being a strong leader or a friendly boss, what am I doing?"

"Gaining impressions."

Pete gave Hank a puzzled look.

"That's right. You're not trying to take charge of the situation; you're not bringing things under control; you're not getting to the heart of the problem—you're just gaining impressions." Hank looked at Pete. "You think you can handle it?"

"I suppose I could try it for a week or two," Pete said, but he didn't sound too enthusiastic. He had a lot of ideas he wanted to make happen, and patience wasn't his strong suit. He spent the salad course in a mental cocoon, and Hank didn't interrupt him. Pete mentally rehearsed five different ways of telling Hank that he had changed his mind. Then he figured out five other ways to do what he wanted to do anyway while still staying technically within the "rules."

But by the time his fish and Hank's chicken arrived, his mind had begun to play around with Hank's suggestion in more positive ways. It was an intriguing notion, something different, and that was worth trying every once in a while. When Pete finally looked up to ask Hank for some detail on how gaining impressions was supposed to work, Hank seemed to be waiting for just that question.

"Well," Hank responded, "which elements in the new job would you say are the most important for you to find out about?"

After they had discussed these elements for a while, Pete jotted down a list of the items he needed to know:

- Who are the key people I work with—above, below, and at my level?
- What really counts with my boss and the company besides the balance sheet and the income statement?
- How much latitude will I have to run my own show?
- How committed is the organization to moving ahead on longer-range technology?

When Pete finished his list, Hank gave him one firm and final instruction: "The idea is not to jump to conclusions based on scuttlebutt. Don't decide what's supposed to be wrong or right about the department or who the good guys and bad guys are. Instead, your objective is to gain impressions about *how* things work." Driving home after dinner Pete pondered the conversation. He had expected Hank to tell him the ins and outs of the organization, but instead, Hank seemed to be telling him to find out for himself.

Pete started his new job a week later and was so busy for the first couple of days that he totally forgot everything they had talked about. What reminded him was his first get-acquainted meeting with the Electronic Publishing Division's marketing manager. He had started to tell her (maybe "dictate to her" would be more accurate, he had to admit) about changes he wanted in her department's reports when he got the impression that her face had turned to stone. He remembered his conversation with Hank just in time to pull out of the demand mode and change the subject.

The next day in the division VP's staff meeting he watched the other people interact without saying much. It looked like the division staffs, especially Marketing, had a lot more influence with the boss than they had in Pete's previous organization where the technical people represented the anointed and everybody else just backed them up. These staffers seemed to have real influence. Listening to them, he found out that there were complexities in the division's markets, including questions about which niches the division could afford to cover before going resource poor.

Pete entered seriously into the gaining impressions process the next morning. He had a meeting scheduled for nine o'clock with one of his subordinates, Steve Wilton, an engineering group leader. Pete had already heard a lot of other people's opinions about Steve—not many of them encouraging. Steve had been a strong insider under Pete's predecessor. He had a reputation as technically arrogant, one of those techno-aristocrats who had surveyed the possibilities five years ago, made his decisions, and now refused to consider any alternatives.

Pete had originally scheduled the meeting to talk about a group of new products under development. He expected a disagreement and had planned his arguments to pin Steve to the wall on some key design trade-offs. But just before Steve arrived, Pete decided to put that strategy out of his mind and instead just gain impressions. His new strategy had an effect.

Without planning to, Pete found himself really looking at Steve as he came into the office. Somehow he didn't look quite as arrogant as Pete had been imagining. He looked intense and nervous. They spent the next forty-five minutes on the review. Pete had expected Steve to argue against his suggestions, and he pretty much did, but Pete didn't push back. Instead he let Steve talk and asked some questions. And there it was, crystal clear: Steve wasn't resisting the proposals because of his commitment to a favorite technology. It was worse. He was digging in his heels because he didn't have enough functional knowledge of the alternatives. He hadn't kept up with the technology. He couldn't possibly lead a change in the engineering group, even if he wanted to.

When Steve left, Pete leaned back and moaned. The department was in more trouble than he had thought. Steve Wilton would have to be transferred and replaced. Hank's gaining impressions idea, he reflected, had spotlighted some bad news, but knowing it early was going to save a lot of time and frustration.

Pete stayed with his new exercise for the remainder of the day. Nothing very startling happened, but he did get a couple of unexpected warm glows, one out of a few minutes he took to stop by his new secretary's desk, just to make contact. He discovered she had a good sense of humor. Later, a couple of venturesome young marketing people stopped by his office and almost shyly welcomed him to the division. He had to admit to himself that he liked the feeling.

During the remainder of the week, Pete met a number of times with his staff, both individually and in groups. He began to gain impressions of their styles and attitudes. In meetings, he also noticed where there seemed to be alliances among them and where there was competitiveness. Once or twice, he caught himself about to take sides with those he agreed with. But he resisted the temptation to spout off, and as a result, heard some interesting ideas from a couple of the more reticent people who had taken a while to warm up.

A few weeks later, Pete and Hank went out to dinner again. All in all, Pete had to admit that Hank's prescription had been worthwhile. He picked up the check.

Don't Just Do Something, Stand There (for a While)

Whether you are sizing up the possibilities and problems of a new job, or taking a new look at the possibilities and problems of an old job, gaining impressions is an application of your awareness skills. Planning and taking effective action (rather

116

than reacting reflexively) requires you to cut through the great number of complicated factors that surround most issues and focus on a few essentials. As either a manager or a specialist, you can determine what those essentials are by asking yourself the following questions:

• *What is this situation really about and what is its significance?* A situation may be a task, a target to be met, a personnel problem, or any other issue that confronts you. The definition of the situation may and often does change as you focus on it more sharply. Pete initially thought that his situation involved convincing Steve that a change in technology was required. By avoiding locking himself into that definition too early (a reflex reaction), he learned that the situation really involved Steve's inability to lead a group that would use the new technology. Judging the significance of a situation means determining whether the situation is a low priority in the context of all the other problems you are living with or a high priority. Obviously, for Pete, this situation was a high priority.

• *What do I want from this situation?* Answers to this question will range all the way from I want to get it over with as soon and as unobtrusively as possible and get on with more important issues, to I want to use this situation as a platform to make an important point (and enhance my reputation). In Pete's case, he wanted to replace Steve with a group leader qualified to guide the engineers into the newer technology. At the same time, Pete had a strong desire to find Steve another job in the company that would better utilize his capabilities.

• *What does the situation want of me?* It's important to name the factors that will define a successful solution to the situation.

117

For Pete, the situation required decisive action within the very near future. At the same time, it called for a solution that would have a positive (or at least not a serious negative) impact on the engineering group Steve Wilton headed, as well as on Pete's own boss.

Of course, most people respond *automatically* to similar questions all the time as they deal with the day-to-day dilemmas of their jobs. The trouble with the automatic approach, though, is that it usually evokes reflex reactions—judgments that are often unconscious, unfocused, and habitual, rather than conscious and deliberate. Sharpening your focus and your awareness usually produces better judgments.

The Treadmill

In an earlier chapter, I pointed out that managing was mostly responding, taking care of what comes up as quickly as possible then going on to the next thing. In many ways it's like running on a treadmill—you run hard in order to stay in the same place. The treadmill isn't all bad. It provides routine, and routine requires repetition, and people usually improve as they practice. The treadmill is also dependable (up to a point), even when it keeps you moving at speeds that almost wear you out. It makes you feel wanted and important (look, Ma, all these people are depending on me), and you don't have to think much.

But I also pointed out that if *all* you do is respond, it's highly likely you will eventually trip up because so much is changing in the larger environment, out there where the treadmill doesn't go. Detroit found that out years ago about big cars and most of

U.S. industry found it out more recently about obsolescent manufacturing processes.

If you want to do well in your career you have to make time for getting off the treadmill and looking around. Even if your ambition is just survival, you have to step outside your routine at least occasionally. It's not that getting off the treadmill will solve all your problems. There is something that can be done about some of them, and nothing that can be done about others. The trick is to know which are which. Or as a wise old rabbi, a Catholic saint, or a Protestant theologian is reported to have once said, "Lord, give me the strength to change what can be changed, the patience to endure what cannot be changed, and the wisdom to know the difference between the two."

One of the best excuses for staying on the treadmill is that your organization is constantly fighting fires and managing by crisis. So what would be the use of getting off the treadmill, even if you could find the time? I've seldom worked in an organization that didn't provide this justification to some extent. But it really isn't a good excuse. Being continually involved in crises really means that your *first* priority ought to be to step off the treadmill and look at the tools and techniques you are using for responding to the crises. Even SWAT teams periodically reexamine their tactics. If you don't, you'll scamper on like that lumberjack, too busy chopping trees to stop and sharpen your axe.

Getting off the treadmill is easy to talk about but tough to do. There is so much momentum to keep you on it. Smart managers build off-treadmill time into their management systems. They regularly set aside a time and place to get themselves and their teams away from the office or plant and its daily grind for some fresh thinking. Then they translate those thoughts into better operations. If you have a boss who makes getting off the treadmill part of his system, you're fortunate. If you don't, there's only one way to make it happen and that's to do it yourself.

Try the Time off the Treadmill exercise to see if you are ready to step off your treadmill. As you try it out, forget about your *shoulds*. Instead, see what *is* for you at this point in time.

Exercise:
Time off the Treadmill

1. Right now, without evaluating in advance whether it is true or false, say out loud: I am willing to step away from the ways I am now doing my job and examine some new ways of doing it. Then after a moment, say out loud: I am not willing to do that right now. Repeat both statements in quick succession several times, just listening to yourself without trying to *tell* yourself which statement is accurate.

2. If you have tuned in to the sound of your own voice and your feelings, you now *know* which statement is accurate for you right now. If you found yourself unwilling to step away, that answer is not necessarily permanent.

3. The best way to change is to start by being clear about where you are right now. So, if you are dissatisfied with your answer and want to go further, get a pencil (or a keyboard), tune in to your spontaneity, and complete this statement, using single words or short phrases: "The two or three conditions that would help me to be ready to step

120

off the treadmill are. . . ." When you are clear about these conditions, you can decide what you want to do about them. When you are ready, the personal strategy and tactics review in Exhibit 6.1 can help you take the next steps.

Opportunities and Obstacles

What to do during your periodic off-treadmill intermissions? Two important elements to examine are your opportunities and obstacles. When you look at your situation, think about opportunities that arise out of current conditions, and those just over the horizon. Can you do some things better, faster, or cheaper? Are there ways to improve your subordinates' satisfaction with their jobs and interactions with each other?

Opportunities are also often connected to words like *stabilize, develop, define*, and *implement*: making a new process more reliable, defining product specifications more clearly, and putting a plan into effect are examples. Opportunities may involve doing something new or doing in a better way something you have been doing: expanding the market for a product that is selling well, improving a process in your department that will enable another department to produce a better product or service, and defining and implementing a consistent system for conducting your business are examples.

Sometimes, it may not seem that there are many or even any opportunities. Just keeping your head above water and meeting your boss's demands may be all you can handle for the present. When that's the case, you are more likely to see problems or obstacles than opportunities. These are the downsides, either potential predicaments or corners you are already backed into. Product quality is slipping. Two of your subordinates who are supposed to be working together on an important project won't talk to each other. Your boss keeps putting off deciding between the proposal you made and the one made by another operating unit. Your two best customers both want deliveries on the same day, and you can accommodate only one of them. But whether you call your situations problems or opportunities, the same questions apply: What's the situation? What do you want of it? What does it want of you?

If your job is like most managers', you probably won't get to implement all your answers to these questions or even most of them. But think of your answers as starting points in the process of developing one or two key priorities. The survey shown in Exhibit 6.1 will help you to think about the prioritizing process. After you complete the survey, it's worthwhile to review your responses with a friend or colleague who knows you well. (You can offer to reciprocate.) When you're satisfied with your answers, consider setting up a meeting to review them with your boss. You can use this survey in working with your subordinate. Ask the subordinate to fill out a copy of the survey, and you fill one out as well *with the answers you would most hope to see in his or hers*. Set up a meeting to compare notes and discuss the survey.

Exhibit 6.1 A Personal Strategy and Tactics Review

NAME _____ DATE _____

The following review can help you and your manager to identify important elements of your job and to discuss ways in which you and your manager can help each other achieve high-level performance in the organization.

Complete the statements below in sufficient detail to be clear but not exhaustive.

1. In thinking about my job and organization, our most important opportunities are:

2. Our most important problems, issues, and obstacles are:

3. The main objectives of my boss's organization to which I can contribute are:

4. The main elements of my strategy for my organization are:

5. The main elements of my personal strategy are:

6. My thoughts about our organizational structure (not people) are:

7. My thoughts about our systems and ways of doing things are:

8. When I think about my staff, both individually and as a group, I believe:

9. The impression I want to make on my staff is that I am:

10. Aside from my staff, the key people with whom I need to relate are:

11. When I think about them individually and as a group I:

12. Other items not covered above that are important to me are:

Take a moment to review your answers above, then complete the following.

13. My one to three highest priorities are:

14. I need to learn more about:

15. What I plan to do is: (When?)

16. The conditions that are most likely to keep me from following up on my plan are:

17. My plans for keeping in touch with what is going on in the organization are:

Notes:
Stepping off the Treadmill

- When starting a new job, don't charge. Taking time to see who the players are, what the environment is about, what you want from it and what it wants of you can make the difference between wasted flurry and precision. Taking time off the treadmill to gain impressions and evaluate situations is important in old jobs, too, even if your only ambition is survival.

- Use your full range of awareness to check out obstacles and opportunities for you, your boss, peers, subordinates, and other major customers. What can you provide that they want? What can they provide that you want? How do you intend to get from the situation you see now to where you want to be? What resources do you have and what do you need? What are your one, two, or three priorities?

- You can't get off the treadmill until you're ready. If you're not ready now, check back with yourself later.

-

CHAPTER SEVEN

Building Mutual Support
Up and Down the Organization

INDIVIDUALS, unless they are hermits or monks, spend their time in societies and, therefore, are required to carve out a reasonably satisfactory way of living among others. Individual adjustments to that requirement are many and varied. They range from relaxed to tense, from highly sociable to very reserved, and so on. If you work in an organization, some relationships are particularly key: those with your boss, with your peers, and if you're a manager, with the members of your staff. This chapter focuses on you and your boss and you and your staff. In a later chapter, I'll talk about you and your peers, especially in competitive and adversarial situations.

There are people who thoroughly enjoy interacting with the boss and others who dread it. Similarly, a manager can find interactions with subordinates to be satisfying and productive or frustrating and fruitless. This chapter deals with developing joint interests that encourage mutual support and positive relationships among organizational levels. That isn't always possible, of course. Some bosses and some employees are impossible, but most are merely human. Significant differences in perspectives exist at different levels of the organizational hierarchy, and

127

if you don't want to be perpetually baffled (whatever your level), you need to recognize these differences.

In the chapter, I will make suggestions for managing managers who don't manage you the way you would like to be managed, and I will talk about ideas for sensing the satisfactions and dissatisfactions of those who work for you, including the uses and weaknesses of attitude surveys.

This chapter is applicable to managers and those who aspire toward managing whether they are oriented toward individualism or not. The core of individualism that runs through this chapter is the requirement that you, the individual, initiate action rather than wait around for someone else to change your environment.

Making Support Mutual

Knowing where he stood was important to Eldon Johnson, vice president of the Structural Imaging Business Unit. He had been in his new job five months and he knew his boss, sector executive George Adamson, had been watching him. From Eldon's past experiences at Globaltech, he also knew that performance appraisals were seldom conducted at the higher management levels, such as his, and when they were, they tended to be awkward. Besides, a performance appraisal wasn't what Eldon wanted. He wanted a mutual discussion of how both he and George could best work together to benefit not just his but each other's effectiveness.

He had casually asked George for a "stock-taking" meeting a few weeks ago, just saying that he would appreciate an informal get-together while he was still in the early part of his job cycle.

George had looked at him curiously for a moment, then had agreed, smiled, and asked if there was anything he ought to prepare in advance. Eldon had said no preparation was needed.

Now, they sat in Eldon's conference room, which was comfortable and out of the constant stream of people and events that ran through Eldon's office. Eldon said, "I thought that getting together like this, early, could help our communication. What I would most appreciate, George, is your off-the-cuff observations on how I've been doing my job. Things you've seen that you like and things you think I could improve on. I'd especially like us to talk about ways I can be of more help to you—what you would like more of, less of, or differently from me?"

"That's all?" George grinned.

"Well, I do have a few requests of you, too, that might help me in my job. Sound reasonable?"

"Seems like a good idea," George said. "Only we both need to remember my comments are based on only about half a year of observation."

"Sure. How about the positives and problems so far?"

"Well, I'll start with your strengths. First, I think you're seen as a strong manager, not just by me and the executive group, but by your own people as well. You also understand the technology of your business well, better than I do as a matter of fact." George smiled, "I get envious sometimes. I remember when I used to be closer to the technology. It was fun."

"I won't disagree. It is fun, but it does get tougher and tougher to find the time to keep up."

"You're also a good businessman, and a good executive. I've seen you handle both good news and bad, and I like your reserve.

129

It's professional. You also seem to care about your people, and I think that's noticed." George seemed to have tapered off. He sipped some coffee.

"How about the other side of the coin?" asked Eldon.

"Well, before I start on that, why don't you tell me what *you* see as your strengths so far?" George replied.

"Fair enough. I guess what I feel best about is that I've brought some order to the group. We were a pretty scattered bunch for a while. That really helped us with our execution on the L114 program. I'm also pleased that we brought the program in on time after being behind. I think I've enjoyed becoming part of the organization and gaining acceptance." Eldon paused. "Sounds like a self-congratulatory speech, but you asked for it. I also think I've recruited some good people into the organization."

"Joyce Prestovich, for one," George commented. "Talented."

"She sure is, and has a good brain for product strategy too."

"Okay," George said, "here are my thoughts about the problems. I'll use the more, less, and different format you suggested. I would like to see you work *more* on your own strategy for the business, and to understand my strategy for the sector better." He paused. "What's your reaction to that?"

It wasn't easy, but Eldon said, "I'll accept that. I've been spending most of my time on internal structuring. I'll plan on shifting attention for a while."

"That's the most important input I have. What do you see for yourself in the problems column?"

"The length of time I've taken for key staffing, and the too little time I've spent on long-range thinking. Part of my trouble is what an old boss of mine used to call my perfectionism. It

130

slows me down. I haven't organized my interface with the corporate staffers as well as I should either."

"Yes, I'll second some of that. I think you are slower to act than you could be sometimes. Maybe that's the perfectionism." George was pretty relaxed by now. He seemed to be considering, then to decide to go ahead. "One other point. I don't usually talk about things like this, but it might be helpful, Eldon. In my staff meetings, it seems to me that when some of your peers bring up their ideas you tend to focus on the weaknesses. In fact, with your background, I think you go into the technology too deeply. It diverts us sometimes from our main course. I would like to see *less* of that in the future."

"Point taken. The next thing I'd like us to talk about, if you agree, is how we can be most helpful to each other."

George nodded.

"You have already been helpful to me and I appreciate it," Eldon said. "You were very open when I first came aboard about the organizational situation. You've also let me do the job without interference. And you've been a good sounding board for me, this session being an example."

"Any additional ways I might be helpful?" George asked.

Eldon grinned. "Well, now that you ask, I sure could use some of your help as a buffer with the corporate manufacturing staff. Some of their demands on my time are driving me mildly crazy. And one other thing, that blast you delivered at me in the staff meeting two weeks ago wasn't too easy to take."

George smiled. "That was after your ten-minute lecture on the fundamentals of nanotechnology, as I recall. But I'll drop a word with the manufacturing staff to tread lightly for a while.

Let's set up some time to talk about strategy. I want to clarify some of the company overview."

"Sounds fine."

"How about dinner one evening next week?"

Building Perspective-Sharing

Some people will read George and Eldon's discussion and sigh, "I wish I had a boss like that." Don't automatically assume you don't. Of course, there are some bosses who are too guarded to get involved in a genuine exchange, and some are unwilling to depart from the formal processes of performance appraisal under any circumstances. But there are more who are reluctant mainly because they anticipate that the appraisal will be a difficult session, in which they will have to prove their points. Preparing and conducting formal performance appraisals is often a disagreeable process for managers. What is different about the meeting between Eldon and his boss is its off-the-record informal atmosphere in which both boss and employee have an opportunity to ask, person to person, for what they want of each other in a low-pressure setting.

Through this approach, George and Eldon have saved time, started to solve problems that could have grown into major irritations later, and begun a pattern of frank exchanges that will probably serve both of them well in the future. They have focused primarily on two factors:

- Eldon's strengths and improvement possibilities, as each sees them

- What each could be doing *more of, less of,* or *differently* that would help the other do his job better

Preparing for a formal appraisal takes a lot of time, especially if the assessments to be delivered are not altogether favorable and the manager feels the need to build a case to support them. Then there's the tension of the formal appraisal session itself. When a manager expects disagreement, or sometimes worse, unspoken resentment, that tension can be daunting. If the manager's task, as is still the case in many companies, is to communicate both a pay decision and development recommendations, the task can become even more unpleasant. None of these points is an argument against performance appraisals. People at all levels need information about their effectiveness, but the environments in which most appraisals are held often seriously constrain or even distort that information.

An informal meeting minimizes the constraints of the formal one. It can be initiated by either the subordinate or the boss. After considering George's preferred style and the company culture, Eldon decided not to ask his boss to do any special preparation for the meeting. But frequently, especially at lower organizational levels, it's a good idea to provide a more specific objectives-centered outline to your boss or subordinate in advance. Exhibit 7.1 shows a suggested format for the informal priorities review.

The advantages of an informal and frank exchange are that channels of comfortable communication are set up. Generally, it is easier to set up these channels early in the relationship, rather than later when there will be more issues in the system, but late is better than never. With nurture, the pattern of

133

Exhibit 7.1 Priorities Review

NAME _____

PERIOD COVERED: FROM _____ TO _____

1. For the period specified, the three most important objectives of my boss's organization to which I can contribute are:

2. The objectives of my job that relate to the above objectives are:

3. The major positive factors and obstacles that will affect my ability to meet my objectives are:

4. What my manager and/or others could do that would help me to eliminate or minimize the obstacles are:

5. Other matters related to my objectives that I would like to discuss are:

informal exchanges can be continued in the future. Also, the earlier potential problems can be spotted, the earlier they can be dealt with.

Another less obvious advantage to developing a relaxed communication channel is its cathartic effect. By encouraging your boss to cover what he sees as negatives as well as positives, you help him get his criticism off his chest early and that tends to release the emotional charge behind it.

Managing Your Manager

Some years ago, in a seminar presentation in 1970, I heard Peter Drucker point out that bosses are human. That may still come as a startling revelation to some people. There are people at all organizational levels, high as well as low, who persist in making their bosses into either bigger-than-life heroes or lower-than-life dunces or villains. (Some, indeed, are, but if you find yourself possessed by either of those inclinations, you might test your perception by asking yourself if you have felt similarly about past bosses? How about your parents and high school principal?) We all carry some residue of our childhood dependencies (and counterdependencies), but getting that residue tied up with the person to whom you report usually won't do either your effectiveness or your psychological development much good. Your boss, like everyone else, has both strengths and weaknesses. Recognizing what they are and how they affect you and your job can be important, but don't expect perfection. And if you are seeing nothing but incompetence, it's advisable to assume, at least for a while, that you might be missing something.

One frequent complaint by employees is that they don't get

as much of the boss's time as they would like. In today's often over-busy organizations, that's a regrettable but inevitable fact of life. And when that limited time is spent in wasteful and confusing ways it makes the effect of these time limitations even worse. There are some techniques that either a manager or a subordinate can initiate to better focus the time spent together.

The most basic technique is to use the three *whats* as a guideline for your meetings. They can save you a great deal of unproductive random wandering. A couple of managers I know have had the three whats inscribed on desk plaques.

1. What is the issue or objective?
2. What do you propose?
3. What do you want from the boss?

If you report to a boss who is not skilled at managing the discussion time you have together, take some responsibility for managing the time yourself (exercising your good sense and sensitivity, of course). Bring along a one-page agenda and let your boss see that you have it. Determine in advance what subjects you want to cover, and be clear about what you want out of each subject. Do you want a decision, information, some additional ideas, support in working with another department?

Don't go in with a barrel of problems to dump on her desk, and do propose solutions to the problems you do bring up. If you think you know what needs to be done, say so. If you are not sure, at least prepare some options that the two of you can explore systematically. Take responsibility for going after what you need. If the boss starts to drift onto a tangent, bring her back. Do it diplomatically, but do it. Allow time for socializing (making contact, as discussed in Chapter Two), but make sure you take care of business.

Learn how your manager operates, not for the purpose of praising or criticizing her style, but of how to best work with it. For example:

- Is your boss a better prospect for action decisions in the morning or afternoon? Closer to deadlines, or with plenty of advance notice?

- Is she a reader or a listener? A concept person or a numbers person?

- What are her hot buttons and sweet spots—the approaches that set her off and the ones that she responds to well?

If you don't know the answers to these questions, discuss them with others you trust and use your powers of observation to find out. Practice your grounding and awareness skills and remember to stay within your self-boundaries.

Keep your boss up to date about what you are working on and, to the extent she is concerned about details, how you are going about getting it done. In part, the information she wants from you will depend on the information her boss wants from her. Provide information she can use easily, in a format that makes sense to her. When you have established your credibility, you can also give her whatever additional information you think she ought to have.

And finally, don't be terribly surprised when you don't always get exact answers or precise directions from your boss. Chances are she doesn't know them herself.

There is an ancient Mayan pyramid in Palenque, Mexico, that visitors are allowed to climb. At ground level, one of the things you notice is the rich variety of jungle plant and insect life that flourishes around the pyramid's base. But because the trees and undergrowth are thick, you can't see very far into the distance. When you climb to the pyramid's peak, you can see for miles and for the first time you notice that there are many other pyramids and ancient temples that surround the area. But you can no longer see the details of the plant and insect life below.

On the organizational pyramid, too, what you notice and pay attention to depends on your vantage point. Yours is different from your boss's and his from his boss's. It's advantageous to find out as much as you can about your manager's perspective. As I mentioned before, don't forget that your boss also has a boss who has expectations of him. Learn what the important requirements are, especially those affected by your own performance. Knowing more about your manager's job can be useful in several ways, including, of course, your promotability.

Overall, think of your boss as one of your important customers. Operate in your job in a way that contributes to his and the organization's success. And make sure it's a way that enables your boss and the organization to contribute to you, too, in learning and growth as well as financially. If you can't find a way to achieve this mutual balance, don't stay around. It isn't worth it.

Finally, as a start toward working more effectively with your manager, answer the questions in the Managing Your Boss exercise.

Exercise:
Managing Your Boss

Answer the following questions:

1. What are one or two areas in which I might improve my understanding and support of the requirements of my boss's job?

2. What are one or two ways in which I might manage my boss better?

Managing Your Subordinates

Most organizations are hierarchical. Whether relatively flat or as peaked as a church spire, hierarchical organizations seem to be the only kind that work in industrial society so far. In hierarchical organizations, there are superior positions and subordinate ones, managers and those who report to them. If you as a manager (or an aspiring one) have so strong an egalitarian philosophy that you choose to deny that rule of the game, you are likely to come to grief, probably sooner rather than later.

On the other hand, if you as a manager think of yourself as endowed with the divine rights of an absolute ruler and choose to regard your subordinates as no more than animated tools for use as you see fit, without regard to their interests and needs, you are also likely to come to grief, possibly later rather than sooner.

Managers come in a variety of types. There are tough, tyrannical ones and gentle, considerate ones, inspiring, charis-

139

matic ones and dirt-dull bureaucratic ones, bold ones and cautious ones. Some threaten, some cajole, and some merely hope for the best.

Earlier, I made the point that the most effective approach to managing is dependent on three factors: the kinds of tasks to be managed, the capabilities and attitudes of the employees, and the natural style of the manager. Most of the important functions of managing subordinates can be summarized as follows:

- Assigning work and specifying outcomes
- Arranging for the equipment, resources, and information required to do the work
- Organizing people into combinations that can best perform the work, instructing them in doing the work, and stimulating them sufficiently to want to do it well
- Tracking the quality of work, assuring that good work is rewarded and below-par performance is corrected
- Assuring that people and departments work together reasonably well, rather than blocking each other

There are three important perspectives on how well you are performing these functions: Your boss's, which I have already discussed, your own, and your subordinates'. Subordinates' views of the way they are managed are significant information and one of the most frequently used methods for gathering that information is the employee attitude survey. The results of such surveys can be useful indicators of problems, but survey information is also easy to misunderstand and overinterpret. For instance, many standard attitude surveys pride themselves on their statistical bases. They usually provide the manager with a score and an analysis of how his score compares to the average scores of managers in other organizations.

In my view, that emphasis is not awfully useful. All the survey results I have ever seen yield scores in some categories that are low enough to be interpreted as a cause for alarm. But the manager's comparative score is less useful than knowing whether the so-called problem area is *important and treatable* in the context of what the manager and his unit are trying to accomplish. For example, in a company in a volatile industry with continual and sudden changes in markets and technology, it would not be surprising for employees to rate their manager below the norm in providing clear objectives. How could he set clear objectives when his own keep getting changed?

Similarly, in a company struggling for survival and concentrating on cost containment, the scores for satisfaction with pay and job security are likely to be low.

The halo effect is another frequently misleading survey phenomenon. Some time ago, psychologists discovered that when people are dissatisfied with one key condition the dissatisfaction tends to spread into other related areas (and sometimes into unrelated ones as well). Subordinates unhappy about their pay are quite likely to be unhappy about the way their performance is evaluated and with their promotional opportunities as well.

But the halo effect has its positive side too. And for you as a manager, it is a very positive side. When you focus attention on improving the key condition, and that attention is experienced by subordinates as sincere and successful, much of the related dissatisfaction tends to go away or at least to diminish significantly. So, if you find yourself on the short end of an attitude

Exhibit 7.2 Employee Attitude Survey

Confidential

Manager Interface Questions

DATE _____

This questionnaire asks you to share your perceptions of how well your manager performs the following functions. Base your answers on your manager's usual day-to-day behavior.

Please do not sign your name or identify your position. Only a compilation of all scores will be given to your manager.

Rate each item below 1 to 9, according to the following scale.

1	2	3	4	5	6	7	8	9
Critical need for improve-ment		Significant need for improve-ment		Some need for improve-ment		Adequate situation		Superior situation

You may make brief comments on any of the items (attach a separate sheet).

To what extent does your manager:

Rating

1. Set balanced goals that are challenging and achievable?   _____

2. Provide encouragement and support to subordinates?   _____

3. Communicate the information needed by subordinates to do their jobs?   _____

4. Measure performance against goals and communicate results frankly?   _____

5. Provide coaching and counseling to improve subordinates' performance? _____

6. Expect and encourage cooperative working relationships between units? _____

7. Deal effectively with internal or external obstacles to organizational success? _____

8. Delegate authority and hold units responsible for performance? _____

9. Lead and encourage systematic and effective problem solving? _____

10. Contribute to and encourage others to contribute to a high-energy, high-morale organization? _____

11. Consider and contribute to the development of subordinates' skills and careers? _____

12. Keep commitments made to upper management, customers, and employees? _____

13. Provide opportunity for subordinates and others to influence planning? _____

14. Provide opportunity for subordinates and others to influence decisions? _____

15. Make fair decisions and recommendations with respect to subordinates' pay, promotions, and other rewards and recognition? _____

16. Stay open to innovation (new ideas and ways of doing things)? _____

17. Hold clear performance discussions with subordinates? _____

18. Deal with performance problems early and appropriately? _____

19. Handle other items not mentioned above? (Write
    them in here, or attach a separate sheet and rate
    each.)

After reviewing your answers above, please complete the following:

20. List the item numbers of the one to five items in this
    survey that are most important to you.

21. Are there any other comments you wish to make?
    Please write them here or attach a separate sheet.

survey, don't try to fix everything. Pick no more than one or two of the most important (and treatable) priorities for improvement and concentrate on those.

The survey shown in Exhibit 7.2 can give you a relatively quick picture of your employees' perspectives on the way they are being managed. My cautionary notes apply to interpreting the results of this survey as well. The best way to use it is to identify items that receive ratings of 5 or lower, call together the people involved, and work with them to select one or two priority conditions to work on.

Notes:
Building Mutual Support

- Encourage informal, cordial exchanges between your boss and yourself, centering especially around what you want more of, less of, or differently from each other.

- Your boss also has a boss. When you understand how your boss operates and the current key requirements on her, you are better able to shape the way your boss manages you. Bosses are fallible; don't expect too much of them.

- There is no single best model for managing. Consider the kinds of tasks (routine or complex), the capabilities and attitudes of employees, and your own natural style in developing your own management approach.

- The results of employee surveys can be misleading if you don't consider their environmental context and the halo effect.

-

PART THREE

ORGANIZATIONS ARE INDIVIDUALS, TOO

PART THREE FOCUSES on the importance of recognizing the individuality of organizations as well as of people. While there are many similarities between organizations (companies, departments, and projects, big and small) there are crucial differences as well, and if you don't recognize an organization's uniqueness, you will miss seeing either the best leverage points or the potential pitfalls for your efforts. Signing up for a catalogue of prescriptions in a ready-made improvement program may waste time, money, and the credibility of management.

This section examines what works and what doesn't in the practical application of participative management and employee involvement. Results are usually dependent on an organization's individual characteristics and needs. I also contrast two kinds of teams, the general inclusion group and the individual initiative network, showing how each serves a different purpose and why

147

these teams need to be thought about, designed, and managed in different ways.

Part Three also discusses conflict between groups (teams, departments, and so forth), which can obstruct or enhance effectiveness. Conflict is one of the natural elements of organizational dynamics. It has potential benefits when properly handled, and potential dangers when your opposition is determined to play hardball. Finally, this section examines attempts to change big systems, discussing why these attempts so often turn out to be more slogan than substance.

CHAPTER EIGHT

Participation Is Not a Panacea

THIS CHAPTER INTRODUCES the concept that organizations are unique individual entities with varied characteristics.
There are organizations in which it takes too long to get
decisions and others where hip shooting is the order of the day.
Ones in which managers don't know enough about the details
and others in which they micro manage. There are old bureaucratic ones that are stuck in habitual ways of doing things and
new start-ups that hop from possibility to possibility without
committing to anything. Disorderly ones and overly ordered
ones. Ones with highly refined systems and others that are
basically primitive. These variations occur even in the same
industry.

Clearly, attempting to apply the same set of prescriptions for
improvement to all of them is dysfunctional. Yet we keep trying.
Later, when I describe the results of many of the currently
popular large-scale organizational change programs, we'll see
some of the unfortunate consequences. It's like trying to cut one
set of clothes to fit all individuals, whatever their sizes or shapes
or the climates in which they live. It can probably be done, but

for any given individual, the results will not be attractive, comfortable, or functional.

If you are to pick one or two ideas that are most likely to yield what your organization most needs, you must know your organization's key operating characteristics and stage of development. Later, I describe specifics, but first, here are some general guidelines, and an example.

- *Recognize the usefulness of management theories and principles and of other organizations' experiences as possibilities, but don't look to them for all-purpose models.* Start with a discriminating attitude that asks the questions, Is this what *we* most need? and, if it is, What's the best way to make it happen in our particular environment?
- *Carefully select a limited number of decisive targets and tactics,* preferably involving (especially in the early stages) a limited number of key people. What you need to remember, even if you have to carve it on a stone tablet, is that *in any organization there are always more good ideas than there are resources and energy to carry them out.* And when resources and energy are below critical mass for making action happen, anemia sets in, and good ideas die slow, painful deaths. People tend to remember these lingering declines even longer than sudden disasters and are less likely to want to get involved in the next good idea.
- *Custom design plans and approaches to fit the character of your organization's key people and culture.* Be sure you have access to enough power, resources, and sustained determination. Changing a culture invariably takes longer than you think it will.

Participative Management—
When and How Much?

Fred Loomis slouched as he walked away from his meeting. He was satisfied with himself but disappointed in his staff. Once again, he had come up with a good solution to a division problem, but his department managers had seemed mostly passive. He wondered how well they would execute the plan.

Fred was manager of Globaltech's Computer Equipment Division. His intelligence, energy, and determination had made him successful for five years. But without intending to, he had become the sole problem solver of his division's major business issues while his department managers had become adequate implementers of the routine programs that the business required.

But a strong new competitor had recently come on the scene, and the division's market share was declining. Fred's boss had sent in a corporate study team to look at the problem. The team's report, delivered a week ago, had faulted the division's slow responsiveness and slow adaptation to market demands. What was not mentioned in the report, but was clear to Fred's boss, was that Fred had conditioned the initiative out of his department managers. Clearly, he had not practiced participative management.

In contrast, three buildings to the west in the Globaltech complex, Ted Reasoner, marketing manager for Globaltech's Information Products Business Unit, had attended a middle-management training program two years earlier and had become a total supporter of participative management. He consistently encouraged his entire staff to participate in setting the

151

unit's objectives and deciding how to reach them. He was firmly committed to full employee involvement, expression of all points of view, and decision making by consensus.

But while issues were broadly discussed and self-expression bloomed in Ted's organization, this approach led to few firm decisions, and little was accomplished. Ted's staff showed plenty of initiative, but took the unit in too many directions, without attending to its most urgent needs. In private, Ted's group complained about each other's "obstructionism," and other departments grew intolerant of their failures to meet deadlines. After a year, Ted was moved to a company staff job.

These two anecdotes illustrate the two sides of participative management and employee involvement, once viewed as a management panacea. Both Fred and Ted had managed to make weaknesses out of their individual strengths. Fred's strength was his personal ability to solve problems, Ted's was his support and development of his staff. Fred's mistake was in using his talent to the point of excluding his subordinates from the decision process. Ted's was in becoming so enthralled by the *idea* of employee involvement that he applied it without careful discrimination.

Ted is not alone. The virtues of participative management, and its variations in which a manager shares decision making with her subordinates, have been promoted enthusiastically over the last decade under a number of designations. How sound is participative management? The answer is that it all depends.

Generally speaking, participative management has three basic theoretical advantages.

1. More heads are better than one. Participation can improve the quality of decision making, especially since

many of those extra heads are closer to the action than the boss is.

2. A consensus decision is likely to be followed up more enthusiastically because people who have a hand in making a decision are better motivated to implement it.
3. Participation in decision making is effective on-the-job training that helps develop subordinates.

There is merit in each of these points. And yet there are times when participative management can be time wasting and counterproductive. If you are a manager or an aspiring manager, you will probably at some time want to introduce some form of participative management into your work group. What makes the difference between an effective and a dysfunctional use of the concept is your picking the right time and the appropriate form. As a manager, if you are selective, you can avoid some of the ditches and detours that frequently plague participative groups. As a work group participant, if you know about the ditches and detours, you can keep your expectations reasonable and your contributions on target.

Precautions

When you are contemplating the adoption of participative management, follow five basic precautions.

1. Do Not Introduce Participative Management When Radical Changes Are Needed Quickly

A participative management approach is not useful in a turn-around situation. Radical changes inevitably involve stepping on toes. Some would-be participators may even be perceived as those who caused the very problems which brought about the need for a turnaround. Beyond the matter of appearances, the old guard may also be defensive of its previous actions, denying responsibility and blaming others for what went wrong. These attitudes can obstruct and distort corrective actions. If your organization needs a radical revision of its structure or processes, it's likely that new technologies will need to be considered—for example, statistical process control. Most group members are not likely to be well informed about these new approaches and may be resistant to them. New, outside inputs will be required.

A major information technology business had been so dominated by its research and development group that it became known in its industry as a "sandbox" for designers to try out their pet ideas. While a good deal of creativity was generated in the organization, very little of it was converted efficiently into new commercial products. The result: new product introductions to the market were consistently delayed and too frequently cancelled. A newly appointed general manager, working with a hand-selected advisory group, recognized quickly that the organization needed a clear change in emphasis. He replaced the director of R&D, reduced the department's size and dominance, and reorganized to enhance the influence of the production organization. Only after these major changes were made, did he solicit members of the "new" R&D department for their ideas about increasing their department's operating effectiveness.

2. It Is Seldom Economical to Build a Participative Team Among Those Who Interact Only Occasionally

Effective decision-oriented collaboration requires open attitudes as well as problem-solving and negotiating skills. These attitudes take time and training to develop and, like muscles, must be regularly exercised if they are to be kept in shape. Participative approaches can be more trouble than they're worth when contacts among those involved are infrequent.

3. Participation Is Only Conversation Until It Is Translated into Action

To work, participative management requires not only sound, well-informed inputs from subordinates but also result-producing follow-through by you as their manager. Unless you have the clout, energy, and determination to carry your group's message up the line, and get the support and resources necessary for successful implementation, think twice. If you don't get results reasonably often, both the participation process and you can lose credibility. As the next precaution illustrates, other forms of involvement may work better for you and your group.

4. Don't Forget That Teamwork Can Be Encouraged Through Other Processes

You can foster your team's involvement at one or a combination of stages in a decision chain. What is important is that both you and your team members are clear about what is expected of them and what is not. The range of possible involvements for team members includes:

- Identifying problems and discussing how those problems are affecting the team. For example, you can ask team members to list the situations that get in the way of their doing their jobs well.

- Developing a list of possible solutions for upper management to review. That way, rather than being called

on to develop one definitive solution, team members are
encouraged to explore options.

- Working out a consensus definition of a problem and
developing a list of specifications for the solution (not the
solution itself). For example, your team might conclude
that a more effective transfer process from engineering
design to manufacturing is needed. Higher management
levels then decide on the particular method or
organizational configuration to best achieve a new transfer
process.

- Recommending the best *ways to implement* a decision once
it has been made, and reporting on post-decision problems.

5. Don't Ask for Participation in a Decision That You Have Already Made

Managers sometimes have strongly held ideas and strong wills
to carry them out. There are times when this singular uncom-
promising vision is essential to an enterprise. When you have a
clear and burning vision of where your organization needs to
go, you ought to get on with it, not pretend the subject is still
open.

In one organization, a senior manager had decided to com-
bine the manufacturing units of three divisions into a single
central function. But in an effort to soften the blow, he didn't
inform his division managers. Instead he held a series of meetings, ostensibly to discuss their views. But whenever alternative
ideas were raised by the division managers, the senior manager
found objections to and weaknesses in their cases. It didn't take
his staff long to figure out what was going on. One of the

division managers resigned shortly afterward. The subterfuge and repeated rejection of the managers' views bothered him more than a straightforward announcement of the reorganization would have.

Participators Are Made Not Born

A manager should initiate participative management only if she has a realistic sense of what it requires and is committed to making it work. When you consider installing a participative approach, be aware that not everyone is born and raised to be an effective participator in decision making. The traditional structures of many families condition some people to play dominant or acquiescent roles, and they carry these patterns into their organizational lives. Changing these roles requires managerial effort and patience.

People need to *learn* to participate effectively. They need skills for the identification, analysis, and solving of problems. To make their decisions work, they also need skills in negotiating, planning, and implementing. These skills can be taught by specialized instructors or by willing and able managers. But doing so requires knowledge, and persistence from you as the manager and lots of practice from your team members as their skills gradually develop.

Organizational traditions, too, can discourage the big-picture thinking needed for optimizing overall organizational performance. Large-scale production, departmentalization, and specialization contribute to special interest attitudes. Work groups concentrate on performing their functions in ways that best serve their own interests, rather than looking beyond to broader company purposes or cross-department objectives.

For people to be effective participators, they have to be better informed than those only required to "do a job." They must understand the background of the issue upon which they will decide. Communicating this information is time consuming. It may also be risky. You need to ask yourself if you're willing, and to what extent you're willing, to stick your neck out if your organization's culture discourages sharing sensitive information—for example, financial data, new strategies, or organizational changes the company is contemplating.

Participative management's shared decision making and feelings of shared purpose do not translate to shared responsibility. It's the manager who is at risk. If a participative decision fails, you usually can't share the blame.

By now you may be wondering whether this participation/involvement trend is for you. My intention is not to turn you away from participative management, but rather to make your venture a more informed one that meets your and your organization's individual needs. If you have seriously considered the benefits and demands of participative management and decided to proceed, consider the following guidelines:

- *Ask your team for their views on issues about which they are knowledgeable.* One manager made it a point to ask his entire staff to identify unmet needs, things they had direct experience with, in the division's management information system. But he did not ask them to design an alternative system, or even to establish its specifications. For those tasks, he hired an external service company to work closely with the MIS manager.

- *Start "experiments" in participation with a relatively small, selected base of volunteers.* Work with people who want to be involved on a few pilot projects until the group has some success. Publicize the results and provide opportunities for others to join the group or to form other groups. Let participation grow organically in fertile areas rather than make a general program of it. To maintain credibility, solicit only the number and kind of ideas you can follow up on and expect to implement.

- *Rather than start with participation on the most critical and difficult organizational issues, start with easier ones.* Tackle the more difficult ones as the team gains experience and ability.

- *Respect the preferences of individuals who are not interested in participating in management decisions.*

- *Regularly evaluate the effectiveness of the participative process.* Find out what works and what doesn't. Don't get caught in the pluralistic ignorance syndrome (trying to convince each other how well the approach is working when no one really believes it).

- *Finally, remember that participation is useful in some situations and not in others.* There is no easy substitute for thoughtful judgment to determine when participation is appropriate and when it's not.

Notes:
Participation

- Broad-scale participative involvement is most useful for gradual, incremental improvement, not when radical change is needed.

- Start participative involvement with easy issues and be sure people have the required knowledge and skills for a successful experience. Regularly evaluate the outcomes of the participative process and adjust it as required to make it more effective.

-

CHAPTER NINE

Creating Teams That Encourage Individual Initiative

THIS CHAPTER SPEAKS FURTHER about work groups in terms of realities rather than wishful thinking. It identifies two kinds of groups:

- *General inclusion groups* (GIGs)
- *Individual initiative networks* (IINs)

When you understand the distinctions between GIGs and IINs and know what you can and can't expect from each of them, you can make better decisions about when and how to use them. Most of the emphasis will be on the IIN, for two reasons: first, because it's been largely neglected by those who write about organizations, and second, because there's an increasing need for the kind of output individual initiative networks can produce. When you face a tough issue that requires a radical rather than a gradual solution, the IIN can help.

General Inclusion Groups

General inclusion groups are based on the principle of participation by everybody involved in the activity or issue being addressed. They include such formations as quality circles, problem-solving groups, semiautonomous work groups, employee involvement teams, and so forth. With appropriate training and direction, as discussed in the previous chapter, GIGs have proven useful for incremental organization improvement. They have also demonstrated significant limitations, particularly if the change required is radical rather than incremental.

David Norton of Nolan, Norton & Co., information technology consultants, who clearly favors employee involvement, nevertheless found in his studies of typical GIGs that they had serious limitations. Even when they were given broad charters, strong encouragement from above, and were enthusiastic, their results were frequently disappointing. In a 1988 report entitled *The Digital Equipment Corporation Networking Case Study*, Norton gives these reasons for GIGs' failures:

- *"Functional myopia"*: a tendency to concentrate on their own organizations and specialties, and to ignore cross-functional interfaces, where Norton believes "the real opportunity for dramatic improvement lies"

- *"Lack of vision"*: a confusion that comes from not knowing where to begin or upon what to concentrate

- *"Executive abdication"*: the "self-preservation" drives and resistance to change of people in organizations, traits that preclude individuals' considering changes that strongly affect people or practices close to them

The experiences of the manager of a development organization who had three separate general inclusion work groups reporting to him also illustrate GIGs' typical problems. These three groups were composed of competent engineers and technicians who were charged with developing recommendations to significantly reduce (by 25 percent or more) new product development time. This goal, which they agreed to, was recognized as important to business survival. But even so, they couldn't seem to make any progress. They seemed to have built their own cages and were determined to stay inside them. There were three main ways in which the groups failed to come to action. Whether you're a manager or just a group member, you'll probably recognize these "techniques."

• *Avoiding the issue.* Their early discussions kept shifting from one subject to another without focusing on specific issues. When a group was encouraged by its manager to select one or two key priorities, the members were reluctant and continued to vacillate among possibilities. Their eventual recommendation seemed as much an abdication as a recommendation; ironically, it was, "Appoint a single project manager with decision making authority."

• *Dispersing solutions.* Group members made few recommendations for *major* changes in procedures or structures. Those that were proposed by a few members got little attention from the others, or were sidestepped. Group members were most engaged and talkative when they discussed who was "at fault" for existing problems.

• *Minimizing change.* After the initial unsatisfactory series of meetings, each GIG was asked to meet on its own to develop specific change recommendations. The quality of recommendations varied among the groups, but even the better suggestions were limited in scope and would not have resulted in anything near the targeted 25 percent reduction in cycle time.

General inclusion group members usually approach their tasks with understandable caution. They may be willing, even enthusiastic, to join in stimulating discussions that invite them to identify their own problems and solutions rather than having solutions imposed by the boss. But that does not mean they are ready to soar to new horizons. More likely, they will choose to trudge through familiar terrain, and only after making sure that the trail is safe. Here again, whether as a manager or a group member, you're likely to recognize the typical patterns.

- Avoid threatening others' interests (and they'll avoid threatening yours).

- Be careful about making proposals that could affect your own job (or the jobs of the people in the group you represent). You may wind up with more work to do, and management is unlikely to relieve you of any of your present duties.

- Avoid the inevitable risk involved in major changes ("nobody ever got fired for buying IBM" was once a popular decision-making truism).

- Stick with the group viewpoint in order to avoid personal discomfort or embarrassment in group discussions.

- When unsure about what to do, delay doing anything by getting involved in discussions about details, semantics, and general principles.

- Don't fix anything that "ain't broke."

GIG participants are, of course, no worse than the members of most groups. They face powerful norms, pressures, and inhibitions. Safety and conservation of status quo are powerful motivations within most social groups. It's also important to recognize that well-trained and well-led GIGs are often able to get past some of these barriers to problem solving. GIGs have been useful in incremental quality improvement and production problem solving in many organizations. But even these useful GIGs tend to produce solutions that are extensions of their current operations, not major innovations.

Individual Initiative Networks

When issues facing your organization require refinements or improvements of existing procedures, trained general inclusion groups can perform well. But, in today's competitive global environment steady, continuous improvement of existing systems may not be enough. Step-function or discontinuous change may be needed. When the issue you and your organization face is critical and tightly time-bound and the decision will involve significant risk, a GIG is probably not the way to address it.

For issues that require new, inventive approaches such as redefining markets or redesigning structures or major processes, it's more useful to think about ways to access *the vision, initiative, and determination of individuals working in voluntary combination to achieve an extraordinary purpose.* This is the individual initiative network.

As a manager, you can encourage initiative networking in your organization. You can be clear in your own mind and with your personnel that you don't expect everyone to participate in everything. You can promote and support selective volunteering. As a nonmanager, you can initiate a key issue task group or participate in one started by someone else.

The individual initiative network is a voluntary association of venturesome individuals who contribute to and support each other's initiatives. For the CEO, the IIN can be a temporary, hand-selected "kitchen cabinet." For the middle manager, the IIN might consist of other managers who have similar interests, a training specialist, a consultant, and one or two subordinates who are enthusiastic about the idea—in short, *people who want to make it happen*. The individual contributor might enlist a few technicians, a marketing specialist, and perhaps his or her own boss.

An IIN is not usually derived from a companywide participation or employee involvement program. Instead, it usually begins organically, in response to a specific current problem or opportunity. The formation of a very effective "technologies and products task force" described by Nolan Norton began when a senior technologist volunteered to work with a company vice president on what both perceived as a critical issue.

IINs are propelled by purpose, and their fuel is a mixture of members' persuasion and power. IINs are often self-organizing rather than carefully planned. They are usually small (so they work efficiently), and have specific targets and short, active lives. They have few of the inhibitory norms of the GIGs. (Often IIN members lack the social sensitivity of GIG members as well, and this can work against them in the implementation stages of their project when cooperation from non-IIN members is required.)

What distinguishes the IIN is the generative, single-minded drive and vision of its initiators, and the transmission of that drive and vision to the other members. The initiators are frequently pathfinders, and they are willing to risk both company money and their personal reputations for the paths they believe in. They may not always be the most personable or accommodating people. They may be egocentric, obsessed, stubborn, and impatient—characteristics that coincide with qualities common to entrepreneurs. But such single-minded, innovative risk takers are essential threads in the overall fabric of successful organizations.

The drive of an IIN leader is demonstrated by the conclusion to the story of the development manager determined to reduce product development cycle time. Disappointed but undaunted by the lack of substantive recommendations from his three GIGs, the manager *personally* took charge of improving cycle time by 25 percent or more. After considerable thought and discussion with several of his peers and lower-level engineers and technicians, the manager good-humoredly named himself "Cycle-time Czar—from product concept to delivery."

From his conversations with (and observations of) people at various levels in the manufacturing function, he recognized a series of important obstacles that were inherent in the disparate scheduling systems used by the development and manufacturing units. In collaboration with the manufacturing manager, he then assigned a small selected group of engineers and technicians (all volunteers) to adapt a key development technology transfer system to conform with the existing system used by manufacturing. This change clarified several previously "invisible" interface slowdowns. Several steps in the overall process were eliminated and others were accelerated. A reexamination of the now clarified process (this time involving GIGs) suggested further refinements. Taken all together, the effort resulted in a one-third reduction in cycle time.

Enhancement Guidelines

There are some steps that you—especially if you're a senior manager—can take to enhance both the GIGs and IINs in your organization.

- *Recognize the uses and limitations of GIGs and IINs and the distinctions between them.*

- *Develop informal inventories of specially skilled people*, such as individual initiators, organizers, and implementers. Build bridges among these people and provide business planning, political skills, and group process training and support for them.

- *Pay attention to the IINs you believe in.* Provide some unofficial budget and ask for short progress reports. When you and the IIN are ready to move the initiative to project status, provide it with a champion who has sufficient clout to carry it forward.

- *Recognize that continually fluid conditions of organizational change are a reality.* While the classic change model has been "unfreeze, change, refreeze," the current era may call for a new model (more familiar to surfers): unfreeze, catch the wave, ride it.

- *Work to minimize envy, suspicion, and opposition* from other group members toward those who volunteer for IINs.

- *Emphasize training that minimizes group-think among GIG members*, especially in the early stages of exploring issues. For example, routinely encourage debates between those who advocate currently prevailing policies and those representing the "loyal opposition."
- *Encourage the personal grounding (see Chapter Two) and self-esteem individuals require* to stand up to majority opinion with both civility and conviction during the debate and deliberation phase of decision making, *and* to support decisions once they are made.

In its early days, U.S. industry's unique strength was said to be rooted in "rugged individualism." If you think of individualism as a return to the days of robber-barons and lone wolves, it's obviously dysfunctional for our time, but if you think of individualism as renewing our heritage of creativity and courage to venture, it's an exciting prospect.

Team Games

On a bowling team you roll your own ball.

On a baseball team you play your position.

On a SWAT team you cover your mates.

On a political team you do your best for the boss.

On a basketball team you do some of each.

There are lots of teams and lots of ways to play and win,

Except if you try to play baseball in a bowling alley.

Notes:
Two Kinds of Teams

GIG

Characteristics
- Involves everybody
- Fits participative management style
- Uses consensus decision making
- Makes incremental improvements
- Arises from a program

Potential advantages
- Stimulates broad interest
- Builds enthusiasm
- Encourages consensus
- Taps more resources

Potential disadvantages
- Creates functional myopia
- Can't decide where to concentrate
- Avoids risks
- Protects members by limiting recommendations

IIN

Characteristics
- Requires directive leadership and selective involvement
- Fits a pragmatic management style
- Uses authoritative decision making
- Focuses on step-function changes

- Arises spontaneously to address important challenges
- Is driven by individuals

Potential advantages (especially for start-ups)
- Enables intense concentration quickly
- Is energized by self-generated determination
- Has built-in power base and motivation
- Explores new paths

Potential disadvantages
- Is stubborn and impatient, single-track driven
- Encroaches on established structures and can complicate, confuse, and slow down work
- Doesn't follow conventional procedures
- Is less sensitive to other people
- Generates less support from those not included

-

CHAPTER TEN

Dealing with Conflict: Negotiating, Winning, and Losing

TUESDAYS WERE THE WORST day of the week. Jeff was away making his customer rounds, and she had to take the kids to school herself. It always got worse from there. Ten o'clock Tuesday morning at the staff meeting, her staff would tell her that Process Development had screwed up again in their characterizations or hadn't delivered on them at all. Then she would need to go over to Tom Lincoln's office and talk to him about it, hating the thought even while she was thinking it.

Sharon Selwyn slouched at her desk, elbows braced to hold her head up. She could see the scene now. Tom would put on his typical ice-face expression and ask her a dozen questions, checking whether she was "quite sure" of her information and implying that she wasn't. And she would sit there and be reminded of her father, who used to do the same sort of thing. And finally, Tom would say that he would look into it. Then he would stand up, signalling that the meeting was over, and she, feeling like a grade-schooler dismissed by the principal, would leave his office. Once she had asked him when she could expect to hear from him. He had mumbled something noncommittal. His office was only across the hall, about four doors down, but it was the longest walk she had to make.

So Sharon decided to complain to Jane Romano, her boss, once again. It was probably the fourth time, but this time, she wrote out a list, and she hoped that would help get some commitment from Jane to do something about the situation. Her list had five points:

1. The Process Development people almost never completely characterize a process.
2. The characterization they do may be meaningful to them, but it isn't useful for design.
3. They pass off guesses as facts.
4. They don't document well.
5. They seem to resent and hinder characterization when we in Product Design attempt to do some of the work ourselves.

Sharon said, "Jane, the Process Development Department isn't supporting my department."

Jane Romano, vice president of Product Design, readied herself. She was familiar with the scream and ream approach, she had used it herself from time to time. Sharon screamed, and Jane was supposed to ream Tom Lincoln, or at least get Ernie Dobbs, Tom's direct boss, to do it. But Jane had a lot of other problems on her mind, and one of the things she least wanted to do at this point in time was get into a hassle with Ernie. But when Sharon laid out her case from the list she had brought, Jane felt she had to respond. Sharon was an excellent performer, and Jane didn't want to see her demoralized. Sharon's department's work was tops. She was a bit weak as a manager, though, especially where head butting was required. She was no confronter.

Finally, Jane said, "Tell you what, Sharon. How about getting a management consultant involved in this, somebody who could help you and Tom and your departments work something out? If you want me to, I'll talk to Tom's boss. I'm pretty sure he'll go along, and if he does, Tom will too."

"Well," said Sharon, who had worked with technical consultants before but never a management consultant, "I suppose that would be all right. I'm pretty desperate."

The consultant was named Jones. When he and Sharon first met, he told her that he wasn't there to dispense expert answers to the problem. "As a matter of fact," he said, "these kinds of problems never really get solved."

"Great," thought Sharon, "then what are we paying you for?" But she didn't say it.

"Actually," said Jones, "that's probably a good thing. The only way to solve them would be to go into a static state, become bureaucratic. I won't try to oversell you," he said. "The best we can all do is to get clear about what's going on that's causing the current frictions, and then see if we can come up with some workable ways to reduce them. If we all learn a few good approaches for handling the problems that will come up in the future, that will be even better."

A full-day meeting was scheduled in a suite of meeting rooms at a nearby hotel. The supervisors and key technical people of both departments were there, as well as Sharon and Tom. Jones began by saying what everyone in the room already knew, that there were serious differences between the two departments that seemed to be getting in the way of both.

"The idea behind this meeting," he said, "is simple. It's to bring out the views that Product Design has about Process Development's work as it affects Product Design's work, and vice versa. After that, we will work at developing some ways of satisfying each department's needs of the other, to the extent that that's doable. My job will be mainly to facilitate the process and to help you all keep on track."

First, at Jones's suggestion, the combined group developed a list of the "umbrella purposes" of their combined work, that is, the group defined what specifications the output of both departments *together* needed to have in order for that total output to be useful for producing the ultimate product. The answers group members developed were not surprising. They all agreed that they needed a continual supply of new processes that could be readily incorporated into the company's new products, making the new products superior to the competition's products and improving their marketability. Next, each departmental group went off into a separate room to develop two lists on flip charts for presentation to the other group. The first list was to display the complaints the department had about its working relationship with the other department. The second list surprised Sharon. It was supposed to predict the list that the other department would prepare. The groups had an hour to work on the first list and half an hour for the second.

Sharon found that the task turned out to be useful in helping all her people share and clarify their perceptions. Jones, visiting each group periodically, also occasionally suggested that the groups clarify a point they were making and be more specific. Compiling the second list turned out to be fun as well as informative. Listening to her people, Sharon heard views that started her thinking that her department might not have a monopoly on justifiable complaints. For example, some people ventured that the Process Development people might be dissatisfied with the amount of lead time Product Design provided to them and might also be less than happy about the specificity of Product Design's proposals.

When the groups reassembled in the larger room and the spokespeople for each department made their presentations, Sharon noticed that much of the tension that had been in the air when they first arrived seemed to have dissipated. Jones laid down a ground rule that there could be no interruptions as each list was presented, except for clarification questions. When the groups presented their lists of predictions, whatever tension was left seemed to dissolve in laughter. Most of the predictions by both departments were right, but a few of them were way off. People in both departments joked that they now had new ideas for things to complain about. Sharon was amazed at how comfortable the atmosphere had become.

After all the lists had been presented, the total group began to discuss the issues. Now the ground rules allowed them to disagree and argue, and many did. Jones helped keep the arguments focused on what one department wanted more of, less of, or differently from the other department. After a while, blaming and accusing declined, and people began to negotiate.

Most people seemed genuinely involved in trying to understand each other's points of view, and a few on both sides were beginning to talk about possible solutions. Jones asked if they were ready to move into the next phase of the meeting: problem solving. They agreed, but by then it was almost lunch time. A soft-drink bar set up in their private dining room gave them a chance to mix with each other for a while before the meal.

Sharon saw Tom standing near a window by himself. She persuaded herself to walk over and talk with him. After only about fifteen minutes in this informal setting, she discovered that what she had been taking for an overbearing and judgmental style in Tom wasn't that at all. Tom Lincoln was shy. They drifted into lunch and sat together. As Tom thawed and became increasingly talkative during lunch, Sharon discovered he was also slightly silly. She almost liked him.

When everyone reconvened after lunch, Jones summarized the morning's work. Then he asked the full group to select the top three issues, those that would most contribute to a more effective working interface between the two departments. After that, subgroups of both supervisory and technical personnel from both departments were formed to identify what each department needed more of, less of, or differently from the other in order to improve operations. The subgroups, each consisting of people who worked closest to one of the issues, did not need to solve the problem, only to establish the specifications of a successful solution. Presentations were made by spokespeople from the subgroups and everyone discussed the ideas. Sharon noticed that, except for a very few people, everyone seemed fully involved in trying to make things work out rather than blaming others for causing problems.

Close to the end of the day, the entire group chose two issues as most important and having the best chance for resolution, and a small cross-departmental task force was selected to follow up and present recommendations to Sharon and Tom in two weeks. Sharon was optimistic when she left the room. She noticed a lot of conversations between people from Process Development and Product Design, and though she couldn't make out actual words, the overall buzz sounded animated.

The next day Sharon told Jane about the meeting, and they both felt encouraged. Jane suggested that Sharon and Tom prepare a joint summary of the meeting and their plans for follow-up, and make sure both Jane and Tom's boss, Ernie, got copies. Jane promised Sharon that she would talk to Ernie about the results at their next meeting and get him invested in seeing that something useful happened. Jane knew Ernie would be just as interested in having one less problem on his plate as she was.

The Nature of Conflict

It's important to keep in mind that conflict in organizations is not automatically a sign of breakdown. Contention is one of the normal dynamics in human relationships, and certainly the typical structures and issues of organizations are fertile breeding grounds for that dynamic. In fact, an organization in which there is an absence of conflict may be an organization caught in what Gestalt psychologists call "*confluence*," where the primary interest is maintaining harmony and order, sometimes at all costs.

Confluence

Geographically, confluence is the place at which two streams come together from different directions and join in a single undifferentiated flow. Confluence can seem an attractive condition for a team. It represents harmony, stability, and a sense of unity. But confluence is only one side of a healthy relationship. If people are to display individual abilities, they require access

179

to the other side as well. The other side is *differentiation*, which includes dispute, turbulence, and divergence. These latter elements are essential to a creative work group capable of responding to change.

At its best, a team, like most other interactive relationships, moves rhythmically from times of stability to times of ferment, from times of unity to times of separation. When a team gets locked into one or the other state and tries to maintain it, that team loses part of its capacity. In confluent groups, people tend to feel comfortable and often complacent. Such complacency frequently accompanies an extended period of business stability when there is little external competition. Bureaucracies, whether governmental or private, performing the same functions in the same ways over long periods, are often complacent and confluent.

Relationships in confluent organizations can be simple or ritualized, but they are most concerned with maintaining the status quo and avoiding discomfort and disturbance. Team members become practiced at avoiding challenges to each other and withholding bad news. A politically correct point of view is fitted to each organizational issue and a good team player is expected to support it. Or as one manager I know puts it, "We all sit around selling each other beer." In smoothly run organizations where confluence has become a way of life, team members automatically identify disturbance as destructive and are reluctant to be seen as troublemakers, boat rockers, or disturbers of the peace. In this environment, potentially valuable critiques and alternative proposals are held back.

Positive Conflict

In healthy, vigorous relationships, confluence needs to be upset periodically. Destructiveness, in the sense of de-structuring, is an essential part of innovation. For something new to be originated, something old must be taken apart. People need to find ways to reassert their distinct points of view, for their own sakes and for the organization's sake as well. When contention is fresh, issue focused, and conducted at a reasonable level of courtesy, dispute submits ideas to testing and helps identify the better ones. When dissent is respected and dissenters valued, they are more likely to regard themselves as a part of the culture than as alienated from it. Loyal oppositions are fundamental to democracies. Even our system of law is based on an adversarial process.

If you want to foster a creative and dynamic environment in your organization, you need to be willing to live with periods of turbulence. You need to recognize and encourage your team to recognize that cycles of harmony and discord, ups and downs, are natural and helpful as long as conflict focuses on issues and is carried beyond complaints to proposals for solutions.

My friend Robert Phillips, a psychiatrist who also consults to organizations, has expressed to me the following four points about conflict:

- In organizations, it's often not conflict but the avoidance of conflict that causes major problems.

- It's extremely difficult to bury conflicts successfully, and the emotional and operational costs of making either formal or informal rules against conflict are usually high.

- Conflicts often represent opportunities for energizing those involved and for creative changes in relationships and processes.

- Typically, the biggest barriers against dealing straightforwardly with conflict are imaginary. People predict catastrophic outcomes, but most often, these predictions are vague and exaggerated (though they inspire real apprehension).

A frequent failing in addressing intergroup discord results from dependence on what Jane identified as the scream and ream route. While this approach is probably better than total avoidance, it's too dependent on the actions of people who aren't sufficiently in touch with the gritty specifics of the issues. Higher-level management on both sides of the controversy understand the issue only as an abstraction. They listen to claims and counterclaims, and because they are not close enough to the work to know the details, they think of solutions only in terms of policies or principles and seldom at the level at which the best remedies can be discovered.

Three Styles for Managing Conflict

Basically, there are three styles you can use to deal with interorganizational discord:

- *Power and push.* Win your point by exerting your authority, dominance, or influence (or your boss's).

- *Hope and hide.* Hope for cooperation; if you don't get it, hide the problem.

- *Give and get.* Communicate your point of view, listen to the other person's, and negotiate a viable way to live together, at least until the next disagreement.

All three styles can be made to work by some people in some circumstances but not in others. For example, if you enjoy competition, you may prefer power and push as your predominant style. If you use your power too often and too high handedly, though, you will find that power and push wears thin after a while. The resentment quotient against you builds up among those you try to dominate, and if they get too fed up, they may decide it's worth the risk to challenge you. No matter how powerful you think you are, there are almost always others in the organization who, alone or in combination, can muster more power. As any number of aspiring tyrants can testify, somebody will eventually "get" you.

Hoping and hiding is a useful tactic if you use it selectively to bypass the battles you don't feel prepared for in favor of fighting the one you have a good chance of winning. If you're not terribly interested or involved in your work or your organizational status, hoping and hiding is a possible survival strategy. You keep a low profile, avoid taking sides, and get your satisfaction outside of work. I've known people who have done it successfully. People who use hope and hide as a long-term strategy typically have limited influence or impact on choices and decisions, but for many of them that isn't very important.

Give and get, of course, is negotiation. On the whole, it's a better long-term strategy than hope and hide. Give and get does not preclude the exercise of power. Power is always present as an underlying element in any effort to resolve a disagreement. But the main focus of the give and get process is to develop a mutual understanding of the issues, to expand the number of options available for dealing with them, and to find an approach that both parties can live with. At best, everybody feels like a winner. If that's not feasible, then at least the loser can walk away with what he considers an honorable peace. What's important in successful give and get, from the perspective of individualism, is that you start the process well grounded and with a clear idea of where you stand and what you want. The following guidelines can help you use the give and get process successfully.

- *When planned actions might not be accepted readily by another organization, involve the other group in the planning at an early stage.* Give group members the background information for your case and plenty of time to consider it.

- *Work together to define and get agreement on the umbrella purpose*—the larger mission to which both departments contribute—for example, a saleable product has to be both functional (engineering point of view) and producible (manufacturing point of view). Ask both your organization and theirs, What do both of us need to do better together?

- *Listen closely to others' point of view and take their interests into account.* Find and point out mutual advantages. Use their ideas whenever you can, and give them credit.

- *When there is disagreement, break it down into a list of specific items on which you and the others agree and disagree.* Also, do not ascribe motives to the other side; their motives are irrelevant.

- *Start negotiations with the easier items first.* Focus on what each side wants more of, less of, or differently.

- *Don't forget the human factors* – people's concerns about status, job security, their images, and so forth.

The Feud

A disagreement had become a full-fledged feud, and Steve Fletcher knew he could lose. The other guy had too many guns. Steve was director of sales, and the other guy was Pat Smith, general manager of the Information Products Business Unit.

Theoretically, they reported at the same level, and Steve had made it a point to act like the equal of the operating GMs. He was convinced that if he hadn't they would have had him for breakfast by now.

As Steve summarized it in his mind, his biggest problem was that his sales force was getting zero cooperation from the Information Products marketing people and, of course, they were giving none in return. Steve hadn't missed many opportunities to criticize Information Products' management among his people, and they were all behind him. Pat Smith was calling customers direct and renegotiating deals to squeeze maximum profit out of every one. He could do it now because they had the product lead on the market. Steve acknowledged that some of the deals Pat had made were very profitable, but Pat wasn't thinking enough about future customer loyalty. And he wasn't helping to improve market share.

Steve had to admit that he had been too intense in their last meeting. They had actually gotten into a yelling match. It was hard not to lose his cool with Pat. Pat had called a regional sales manager a liar to his face and that manager had later quit. When Steve told John Drikes, their mutual boss, about that, he hadn't drawn much sympathy. John said the manager's quitting had been no great loss.

Steve had been concerned enough to ask advice from his father-in-law, whom he considered a pretty seasoned executive, on how to handle the situation. Based on what he had said, Steve decided to try a different approach. He set up another meeting with Pat after getting John's approval. The approval had been lukewarm at most. John had suggested to both of them together that they try to get their issues straightened out. In Steve's view that wasn't much, but from John, who almost always stayed out of conflicts between his subordinates, it was a start. Steve would have liked a more active endorsement, but he suspected that if he pressed John too hard to choose between them he would be the one that lost.

Now, in their second discussion, Steve put his case as calmly as he could to Pat. He said, "Pat, Sales has zero authority now to quote business to customers. We have to check first with one of your area marketing people, and usually the guy is a junior type. We are losing market share daily because we are paralyzed. Our pricing is noncompetitive because we're basing it on maximum profit rather than our marketing goals."

Pat came back at him quick and hard. "How do you expect me to give you pricing authority, when your salespeople never tell the truth? The only one who is reliable in that whole department is Joan McCrane."

"Who doesn't tell the truth?"

"Lambert, for one."

"That was a mistake. It wasn't intentional."

"So you say."

"Pat, the salespeople are convinced that you're stereotyping them, and the whole salesforce is feeling it; even our distributors are affected. We need more authority to operate. You've pulled back our ability to allocate product, even to decide channel of sale. That's not normal for a salesforce in our industry. Something has to be done soon, or I'll lose some of my best people."

"You say I'm stereotyping them; what about the way you have been misrepresenting me to them? I've heard all about that. You're undermining me and my marketing group." Pat didn't wait for a response, he just continued the dump. "You had an assignment to renegotiate a basic agreement with our distributors on prices for this year. You were supposed to do it in January, and you didn't do it until July. That cost us three-quarters of a million dollars. And a couple of the contracts haven't been done yet."

"It wasn't as simple as that. We had to lay the groundwork. We couldn't just load it on them. Besides, I never said I could do it all by January."

"That's another problem, getting you to make commitments. No one can ever pin you down; you always put your own English on a commitment and it comes out different."

"We could have lost those distributors if we hadn't held their hands."

"So you say."

Steve stood up, took a deep breath, and walked to the window. Then he turned around. "Okay," he said, "obviously you and I have been seeing a number of things differently. What I'd like to do is look to the future and see if we can work something out that both of us can live with. Let's see if I can summarize the major complaints you have. Then I'd like to take the list with me, maybe talk to some of my people about it, and come up with a proposal to you. Does that sound reasonable?"

Pat seemed to calm down some, but he was still a little suspicious. "First, let me hear your list."

"Okay." Steve referred to his notes. "One, you don't think the information you get from my organization is reliable. Two, you believe some of the things I've said are undermining you and the marketing group. Three, you don't think I make or stick with commitments I make. Are those the main ones?"

Pat looked surprised. He hadn't expected to be heard so clearly, or that Steve would be so direct. He said, "Right." And he agreed to another meeting to discuss Steve's proposals.

They met again a week later. After some brief preliminaries, Steve said, "On item number one, I've had this list of the main forecasts and reports that Sales transmits to your organization drawn up. I've asked Joan McCrane to review all the data and to guarantee the accuracy of each item, except, of course, the ones we both agree are speculative and can't be nailed down in advance. On item two, I guess you'll have to take my word for it that there won't be any undermining from me. And as for item three, for the foreseeable future, I'll give you my commitment in writing, by memo."

Pat didn't say anything for almost half a minute, then he nodded. "Well, that's a start. I'll take a wait-and-see attitude at this point, but it's a start."

"Okay." Steve decided to play his other card. His father-in-law had suggested that he try it if he felt they were making some progress. "Now I'd like to cover the other side of the deal. Willing?"

"Go on."

"Just to look at the other side, what, in your opinion, does the Sales organization need from you?"

Pat seemed to consider for a while, then he shrugged and seemed to decide to go ahead. "Mostly responsiveness from me and my organization so you guys can do your job—the things you're always asking for, delegation on pricing, delivery commitments, and so on. I guess another thing would be for me to quit trying to torpedo you with John." He grinned, and it reminded Steve of a wolf who was just about to eat. "What the hell, I'm willing to give it a shot, not all at once, mind you. We'll take it a step at a time, see how it goes."

Sometimes Things Don't Go Right
Even When You Do Right

This story, alas, did not have a happy ending. Not all interface issues are susceptible to reasonable resolution, or even treatment. The truce between Steve and Pat lasted about three months, but it eventually broke down and a sniper's war started up again. A few months later, Steve left the company. Pat lasted longer—until his division lost its technological lead. After that, many of his customers went to the competition. In a year, he was fired. The moral: if you don't hold the cards, you can lose, even if you play the hand well.

Notes:
Trouble Across the Hall

- Conflict is a normal part of organizational interaction. Avoiding it can hide important issues and perpetuate dysfunctional underground feuds. A policy of suppressing or eliminating conflict can paralyze creativity in an organization.

- Conflict can be destructive or stimulating, depending on how it is handled. Obstructionism, repetitive problems, blaming, personal antagonism, and deviousness are sure signs of dysfunctional conflict. Conflicts often are opportunities for energizing those involved, and when catastrophic imaginings about conflict are made explicit, they frequently turn out to be exaggerated.

- Using dominance as the exclusive mode for resolving conflict tends to build backlash. Processes that involve negotiation and that focus on the joint satisfaction of both parties are generally more productive if the parties have continuing relationships.

-

CHAPTER ELEVEN

The Real and Unreal Particulars of Large-Scale Change

THIS CHAPTER is about large-scale change, the kind that involves whole companies or major parts of them. Whether you are a senior executive, a middle manager, or an individual contributor, if you work in a large organization, you will likely be involved in a large-scale change program sometime soon in your working life. And you will face the question, How seriously should I take this thing? The more you're aware of the options, the better the decision you can make about whether to coast with the program until it passes or work for its success.

If you're a senior manager who is involved in selecting, designing, or steering a large-scale change program, this chapter is especially addressed to you. Its first and most important point is *make sure you understand and are willing and able to provide the resources in money and time that your program will require*. I will also recommend that instead of announcing the new program to your whole organization, you consider starting with a few less vast tryouts first and see how they go. The underlying principle in dealing with planned change, the biggest and most complex aspect of organizations, continues to be that individualism counts. You need to focus on the particulars.

Life of a Change Czar

Studying himself in the bathroom mirror, Bernie Quince thought he was looking older. As he lathered his face, he examined the lines around his mouth and believed they were getting deeper and beginning to develop side lines that attached to the main ones, looking like little tributaries. He remembered the conversation he had overheard in the men's room almost four weeks ago. It wouldn't leave his head. Two department managers he knew only slightly were talking about him and his new job. One of them said, "What do you hear about Bernie Quince taking on the Distinguished Service Program?"

"You know what they're saying?"

"What?"

"Bernie was a really good operating guy, so they staffed him."

The other department manager chuckled. "I heard somebody say that they pulled him up onto corporate staff because he's black and smart and he'll make a good impression."

"I doubt that. There are a dozen or more blacks at corporate, and Globaltech already has a pretty good track record on affirmative action."

"Well, anyway, I hope the guy remembers his operating days now he's breathing that rarefied staff atmosphere. Hope he remembers the time and motion it takes to fill out all those reports those staff guys keep inventing."

"Yeah, show us some mercy and not load even more garbage on us poor grunts."

"From what I hear, the company may be out to win one of those prestige awards."

"If they are, we're doomed. Those things require mountains of paper."

The department managers had finished drying their hands by then and left. Bernie felt a little guilty about his unplanned eavesdropping, but their conversation had explained a lot to him—why his friends were looking at him peculiarly and asking him strange questions about what he had screwed up on so badly that "they" were making a staffie out of him. When he explained that he actually wanted the Distinguished Service director job, most of his friends had looked skeptical.

Now, as he pulled the razor down his cheek, he wondered how smart he had been to take the job. Everywhere he looked in the organization, he found skepticism, sometimes even cynicism, about the program.

"Damn," Bernie said. It was 6:10 A.M., and he had just nicked himself with his supposedly nick-proof razor.

At 9:30 A.M., in a Globaltech conference room on the tenth floor, Jake Collins stopped Neil Morgan before he got through the door and motioned him back into the now empty meeting room. "You heard?" he asked gloomily. "They're starting a 'Distinguished Service' program in the company. As if there isn't already enough peripheral junk we have to contend with."

"It was only a matter of time," Neil said in his soft Carolina drawl, "everybody's doing it. The government's been pressing on the contractors, and they've been pressing on the subcontractors."

"They asked me to join the steering group. You think it's a boondoggle?"

"Be philosophical, Jake. Just remember, this too shall pass, another program of the month sliding down the sluice."

"Sure, but in the meantime people could be wasting more time on a whole new set of information meetings and organizational meetings and who knows what other kinds of meetings, and we'll be buried in piles of administrivia—forms and reports up to our armpits. And the contribution to effectiveness, which we really do need to improve, will be next to zilch."

"Such is the wisdom of the powers that be, old buddy. I imagine our esteemed CEO will provide us a rousing opening speech, then Bernie Quince will come visit us once or twice, and then he'll turn the whole bundle over to the Human Resource folks to handle." Neil smiled like a coyote in a chicken house.

Jake looked at his watch and started for the door. "I have a ten o'clock with the Distinguished Service steering committee. Maybe I can help to keep this thing from getting too elaborate." He stopped, as though a new thought had struck him. "Who knows, maybe we can even do something useful."

"Wouldn't that be something," said Neil.

Obstacles to Change

The idea in this chapter is not to discourage quality improvement processes or any other organization improvement efforts. Clearly, high-quality goods and services are a basic requirement of effective international competition. But for the sake of perspective, it needs to be remembered that there have been a goodly number of improvement programs in the past: zero defects, management by objectives (MBO), management by results, zero-based budgeting, excellence, culture change, total quality management, and others. Some were well conceived and packaged, but the programs yielded disappointing results in many companies, as shown, for example, in studies by the Rath & Strong and Arthur D. Little consulting companies (reported in the November 30, 1992, issue of *Business Week*).

Rath & Strong found that only 26 percent of the programs it examined "rated an A or a B" and "gave more than half of those initiatives Ds and Fs." Arthur D. Little found that only 36 percent of companies it surveyed believed that their quality programs significantly improved their competitiveness. A two-million-dollar study of "quality programs" in 584 companies in the United States, Canada, Germany, and Japan was conducted by Ernst & Young and the American Quality Foundation from 1990 to 1991. They tried to find out why so many programs didn't work. The reasons will not surprise readers of this book.

- Unsuccessful efforts tend to be diffused across the board rather than focused on a small number of decisive changes.

- Insufficient thought and attention are given to the particular company's stage of development and individual needs—what's most important and most likely to work.

- Some "remedies," such as benchmarking (identifying and imitating your best competitors), are useful in some organizations and worse than no action at all in others.

- The use of "employee teams" is considered essential in most programs, but (as discussed earlier in this book) they are useful only in some cases.

Packaged programs, though they usually include worthwhile objectives and techniques, are frequently based on general assumptions about what's wrong with organizations and what to do about it. Not many doctors would prescribe treatment before they had examined a patient's specific complaints and prioritized their seriousness. Not many mountain climbers would take on a serious climb without estimating the best route to get them to the peak. You need a comparable diagnostic process for your organization. Genuine value added (as contrasted to great slogans) is most likely to come from a small number of concentrated efforts that address the individual obstacles and opportunities most important to you. Admittedly, identifying those particulars takes a lot more time and effort than climbing on the bandwagon of a prepackaged program.

The Hawthorne Effect Revisited

In the mid 1920s, Dr. Elton Mayo and the management of the Hawthorne Works of the Western Electric Company became involved in the classic productivity study of all time. Thinking that the keys to productivity improvement were the physical conditions of employees' workplaces, they began a series of experiments in which they varied the illumination of work areas. They found that each time illumination levels were raised productivity went up, and they thought they had confirmed their hypothesis. But to test their findings, they lowered the illumination levels, and a curious thing happened. Instead of declining, productivity continued to go up.

What was even stranger was that in a control group that management worked with, where *no changes at all* had been made in illumination, production also rose. It took a long time for Mayo and his group to come to their ultimate conclusion: it wasn't the lighting that mattered. It was the psychological stimulus. The workers who had been chosen to participate in the experiments had suddenly become important people— people to whom both Mayo and management were paying rapt attention. They were being talked to and listened to.

It turns out that the Hawthorne effect is not so different from the halo effect discussed in Chapter Seven. *Anybody or anything that management pays attention to is going to be stimulated (for a while)*. What that means in the context of improvement efforts is that when management announces a new philosophy, orientation, or thrust it is likely to be listened to attentively by employees. In these days, when employees have been subjected to so many more management pronouncements than in Mayo's time, they may react positively or negatively, questioningly or skeptically, but unless management has used up its attention-getting potential (on too many programs-of-the-month), employees will pay attention. It is important not to squander that attention on frivolous starts, and not to let it deteriorate through subsequent neglect.

If you are the senior executive responsible for a major change effort, before you decide on the scope and style of your organization's effort, make sure you have asked yourself and other key leaders how much time and energy you are willing and able to give to that effort. If the answer turns out to be "not enough," trim the vastness or don't start.

Essentials for Change

Improving the ways organizations operate is hard work for everybody from the CEO down. There are two fundamental prerequisites.

- *People have to believe that change is really necessary.* If people who will be affected, including those at the top of the organization, are not convinced there is a genuine need to do things differently, they will continue to do things as they always have, even if they have to pretend otherwise. In one chemical company, I interviewed a dozen foremen about their reactions to a quality improvement program that the company had been conducting for about eighteen months. After I assured their anonymity, they told me that the program required them to produce a quarterly quota of improvement projects. When I sympathized with the difficulty of doing that, several foremen grinned and informed me that it wasn't difficult, because one of their number was "a very good writer," and he had taken on the job of writing up extra reports each period for any foreman who needed one. These reports were, in some cases, based on elaborations of work the foremen had been doing before the program started. In other cases, which the foremen told about with particular glee, they were pure fantasies.

Only if managers can convey a clear, convincing picture of the nature of the need and a plausible approach to responding to it are people likely to mobilize productively. Pep talks are useful only if they are accompanied by actions that demonstrate you are serious.

- *Top management must be in it for the long haul.* Belief in the effort and active participation by those involved isn't sufficient. No manager, at any level, can afford to abdicate leadership even after the effort is well started. The newly established targets and processes for attaining them need to be integrated into the business's regular ongoing procedures. And since mistakes inevitably will be made, management also needs to be prepared to live with the rough period that is part of any transition from old to new ways. Patience and persistence are essentials.

How to Do It Wrong

- Come up with a vast program to change everything all at once.
- Pick the highest-priced and/or most popular package in your industry and then follow it by the numbers.
- Turn the program over to staff people and consultants to run.
- Be in favor of OP (other people's) change but don't take the tough step of examining and changing your own processes first.

Starting the Action

Bernie Quince had asked for and spent more than three hours with Globaltech's chief operations officer, Bob Claridge, before accepting the Distinguished Service director's job. Bob had actually called the position the Distinguished Service Czar. Bernie had also talked with each of the executive group managers. Mostly, he had explored what their vision was for the effort. He also did some testing for their commitment, what they wanted from him, and what they were willing to give in support. As best he could tell, almost all of them were serious about it. He read Dan Valowski as negative, though old Dan didn't come right out and say so, and he read one or two others as not really caring much one way or the other. But Jake Collins, who had started as a skeptic, was now positive, as was Jane Provder, and Bernie had a lot of respect for both of them.

COO Bob Claridge was frank. He said he had talked the idea around, not just with the executive group, but with some of his old contacts down the line. He and the executive group had decided the company would develop its own approach rather than install the program presented by a consulting firm a few months earlier. At the same time, Bob didn't want to spend time reinventing wheels, so he suggested Bernie could confer with these consultants and any others he chose and use their services however he saw fit. There was also budget to support the effort.

Bernie and Bob decided jointly that Bernie should start with a pilot project. After asking some pointed questions, Jake had volunteered himself and his group, or any part of it, for the project. It was a good selection. Jake was interested, a skilled manager, and had a relatively self-contained business. They agreed that, if after three or four months the work with Jake's organization looked promising, they could begin to spread out to other parts of the company.

Jake started by forming an unofficial "kitchen cabinet" to act as a sounding board for him and Bernie in the early stages. He mostly enlisted people at various organizational levels who were favorable to the idea and whose opinions he respected. He also included Neil Morgan, because Neil was another naturally skeptical guy but not a rigid one. Jake made it clear that anyone who didn't want to participate was free to decline. Only one person did. Jake and Bernie both asked Bob Claridge to sit in on the kick-off meeting of the kitchen cabinet, and he accepted.

200

Jake's division had just gone through two difficult years. They had cut two product lines and cut back their work force by more than 25 percent. The reductions were completed now, and it was time to turn the division around. Jake wouldn't have started the effort otherwise. He knew it would have been a sure failure if he had begun it in the midst of reductions when people were anxious and concentrating mostly on survival. But the business was now trimmed down, and it needed a cause around which to remobilize. Jake told Bernie that he was going to meet with his top team to start their planning, and he asked Bernie if he wanted to sit in. Bernie said he did. The meeting was a long and intensive one.

A Clear Need

Jake was quiet and listened to the discussion without venturing his own views for longer than was usual for him. Finally, he spoke: "What seems pretty clear to me is that the division has been through a very rough two years. We have all felt it. Now we're trimmed down to the core businesses that we'll go with for the next five years. But what's also clear is that we can't just go ahead with business as usual from here on. We need to get better, and we need to get faster. If we don't, we will be facing the same kind of disaster we just came out of, and I'll tell you, ladies and gentlemen, I for one don't need that. It gives me too many gray hairs and sleepless nights."

"But Jake," Saul Chu, his production manager, interrupted, "we're making do with a work force that's 25 percent smaller. Isn't that enough productivity boosting for a while?"

"No, Saul, I don't think so. If we stop here, I think the competition is going to eat our lunch. Not in one big gulp, as

201

they did on our two now departed product lines, but a nibble at a time."

Connie Bernstein nodded hard. "I agree. We're facing a volatile market for the next several years. Customers are getting more demanding, and competition is going to be fierce. What we have to do is to make sure that all our people, at all levels, understand that and believe it."

"Right on," Vic Marquez, the divisional marketing manager, said. "We need to concentrate on adding customer value."

Internal Customers

Jean Ashburn hadn't said much in the meeting up until then. She was a naturally quiet person, but when she did speak the rest of the staff usually listened. "I think we need to expand our thinking about what we mean when we talk about our 'customers.'" She had their attention.

"Meaning?" Jake asked.

"Meaning that we're not just talking about the people who ultimately buy our products. Relatively few of us deal directly with them, but just about every person in this organization has *internal* customers."

"You mean the people who use the output another department produces?" Jake asked.

"Right. I believe we ought to be concentrating just as hard on producing outputs that meet the needs of internal customers as we do on external customers."

"Good point," Saul agreed, "but how do we do that?"

"Let's hold off on the hows till later, Saul," Jake said. "For now, let's just register the idea as a good one."

"Yeah, but we have to remember that most of our people are

operating with pretty full plates. I get cold chills when I think about piling additional things to do on top of them."

Nonessentials

"This probably isn't going to make me popular." Connie Bernstein hesitated, then plunged ahead, "but I think that some significant fraction of what many of our people are doing may not need to be done. It's not essential."

"That's ridiculous," Saul blurted. "We already carved all the fat out of this organization."

"I know people are busy, but what I think most of you have noticed is that we haven't been crippled by the cuts anywhere. Productivity has actually gone up. I have a feeling that if we could find a way to identify nonessentials there would still be lots of them around—things people have been doing for a long time out of habit but that are not all that useful anymore." She smiled, "I have to admit I could find some of those in my own job."

"Well, I'm sure you must be the only one around this table who can say that." Jake grinned and a few others did too. "The thing is, the only place to find those kinds of nonessentials is at the place they're being performed. That means those that are performing them have to do the identifying. I'm not sure our people feel secure enough to do that. They might feel it would jeopardize their jobs."

"Well, what if we guaranteed that nobody would lose his or her job or pay grade?" Connie said.

"And what if we told them in advance that this was a first step and we needed to get rid of the nonessentials so that we could all concentrate harder on the essentials?" Vic Marquez added.

People Considerations

The group discussed Connie's idea for some time, then B. J. March, the division's human resource director, spoke. "These things we've been talking about are important," he said, "but what's missing is the people element. We haven't said much about consideration of their needs."

Jake waited to see if one of the operating people would pick up on B. J.'s point. But it was Jean who carried B. J.'s comment to a more concrete level: "The people who are still with us are our best ones. They have the potential to really make a difference, and I for one think they will want to. In return, I think we have the responsibility to provide interesting and challenging work for them and the kind of training they need to do it well."

B. J. agreed vigorously: "And to support them in building the right kind of environment where people are given real consideration when we make business decisions. We also have the responsibility for helping them get rid of roadblocks in their way."

"To do that," Jake said, "we need to know where those roadblocks are."

"And to do that," B. J. added, "we need to ask them."

It was turning out to be a long meeting, but Jake was feeling good about it. He had two pages of notes, and he observed that most of the others were taking notes too. He calculated that it was time to shift a notch and start talking about action proposals.

Starting with Ourselves

"I think that before we begin to implement anything lower in the division, or even to talk about this, we ought to start an experiment with ourselves as the guinea pigs," Jake suggested.

"What kind of experiment?" Saul seemed a little dubious.

"Well, Bernie suggested to me that, whatever we do with this effort, we ought to try it out at the top and see if it works. If it works, fine. If not, we can see close up where we made mistakes, and we can correct them. That way, when we move the effort down the line, we can provide advice that's based on our own experiences, rather than making this another case of wisdom-passing from the head-shed to the peasants." He turned to Bernie Quince. "Did I say it right, Bernie?"

"Couldn't have said it better myself," Bernie said.

Vic turned to Bernie. "What do we call this program, Bernie? I hear that the company name is Distinguished Service. Do we have to call it that in this division?"

"You can call it anything you all decide on, but I hope you won't call it a program. At this point, what we don't have and don't want is a package of standard operating procedures. My office has a number of ideas and techniques that we can make available to you, but which ones you use depend on what you and your organization decide is right for you to focus on."

"So," Jake focused again on next steps, "based on the notion that we're tailoring our own effort and on the ideas I've heard in this meeting, what I suggest as a start is that each of us, including me, picks a personal goal that focuses on increasing value added to our customers, especially our internal customers, and that eliminates something nonessential in the work we do. Any disagreements?"

There were none, and they spent the last half hour of the meeting agreeing on the details.

Making It Work

Jake Collins and his staff continued their series of meetings over the next several months. They discussed and eventually agreed on guiding principles for the change effort. They worked hard at going beyond an endorsement of motherhood and apple pie to specifics that seemed to fit their own organization. The principles were later used as starting points in a subsequent series of meetings with all levels of division management. After the comments from lower levels, the principles were modified somewhat but not changed significantly.

Based on his experiences with Jake's organization, Bernie Quince developed the following set of four generalizations that he encouraged other Globaltech managers to consider carefully as they determined the shape of their own organizational improvement efforts. The generalizations focus primarily on managers' orientations rather than their specific techniques.

• *Don't preach it until you have practiced it.* Perhaps most important, the effort should begin with intensive discussions among the top management team. The team needs to commit itself to a long-term process and be willing to start with themselves. A useful way to screen an idea is to agree that only if top managers can make it work among themselves should they extend it to the rest of the organization. After exploring a range of options, Jake and each of his staff chose a personal approach to change. In most cases, the choice was based on changes recommended by their subordinates (one set of internal customers). One manager completely changed his system for scheduling individual and group meetings with his staff. Another mandated a drastic reduction in the number of approval levels required in his organization. A third agreed to delegate to project managers authority for decision making that he had previously reserved to himself.

• *Tell them what you think, ask them what they think.* After the top team discussions in Jake's division, another series of meetings was initiated between the top level and the next level of managers. Those in both groups shared their understandings of what the division's guiding principles meant, and how well or poorly the principles were currently being met. In these open and often confrontational sessions, both levels of management were strongly encouraged to express their views and to listen to the views of others. Similar meetings continued with all levels of management and supervision, and with other employees through a series of lunch meetings.

The issue of choosing a name for the group improvement effort came up again in these meetings. After discussing it, a consensus arose among both senior and middle managers that the absence of a title was an advantage. The effort would then become known by what it was about and what it accomplished rather than by a predetermined label.

• *Lead by example not preachment.* The principle of leading by example was adopted as the way in which the change message would be spread through the division. Rather than lecturing, managers concentrated on their own understanding, acceptance, and personal experience with the change effort. They learned firsthand how to make it work and let that information cascade to the next lower level.

• *Don't hype it, spike it.* Jake Collins and his team believed that avoiding hype and a fad image was crucial. Other improvement programs introduced in past years had suffered short lives and had negligible impact. Jake knew there would be considerable skepticism among employees. The top management team decided to take a gradualist approach, extending the effort at first only to units that volunteered and felt "ready"—a pull rather than a push approach. Implementation started with pilot projects that allowed for mistakes, learning, and restarts. When the patterns for success were better known, they were gradually extended through the division. No attempt was made to carry the effort down the levels uniformly. Instead the effort was "spiked" into critical functions and interfunctional processes when that made most sense for accomplishing particular goals. Communication about the effort in its early stages was mostly by word of mouth, and the selling was done by those who had been involved in successful experiences and, for learning purposes, unsuccessful ones as well.

Leaders and the Led

Major change requires leadership—a vision of where you want to be in the future (a *different* place) and the power, patience, and persistence to stimulate a number of other people to move there with you. It's not the same as managing an ongoing function where momentum is already in place and you only need to make adjustments to keep on track.

James MacGregor Burns, a historian, activist, and advisor to three U.S. presidents, first used the term "transformational leadership" in his 1978 book, *Leadership*. He contrasts transformational leadership with the more prevalent "transactional" style: "Transactional leaders approach followers with an eye to exchanging one thing for another (e.g. jobs for votes). . . . The transactional leader recognizes and exploits an existing need or demand in his followers. But beyond that, the transforming leader looks for *potential* motives in followers, seeks to satisfy higher needs, and engages the full person of the follower. The result of transforming leadership is a relationship of mutual stimulation and elevation that converts followers into leaders and may convert leaders into moral agents."

Few managers in Jake's organization would be comfortable thinking about themselves as transforming leaders, especially in the role of moral agent. What they were interested in was keeping the division alive and, if possible, building it into a winner in its industry. It's in the culture, and possibly in the nature, of most U.S. managers to speak of "practical" matters. Nevertheless, in some ways, Jake and his managers did contribute to the conversion of followers into leaders. The conversion began, as the best conversions do, with themselves, when they decided that they would step off the treadmill of their past and view their world in new ways. It continued as their example encouraged others to do the same. The division's effort did indeed generate widespread stimulation among the organization's people and perhaps even some elevation.

Notes:
Big Change

- Large-scale change efforts are difficult and slow. They compete against pressure for short-term results, vested interests in keeping things as they are, and inertia. Packaged change programs are usually not adequately tailored to a particular organization's specific needs and opportunities. Senior management often seriously underestimates the effort required and the *years* it takes for implementation.

- To gain employee support, employees must believe that change is really needed. For real value added, managers' involvement needs to be highly focused rather than generalized, and senior managers must sustain commitment (not pass it off and forget it).

- Managers do better when they lead by example, not preachment. Starting at the senior management level, they must test for what works by personal experience. This way, managers build their knowledge for later guidance of lower levels.

-

PART FOUR

CUSTOMS OF COMMAND AND ARTS OF THE POSSIBLE

POWER AND POLITICS are necessary aspects of organizational reality. This section looks at the question of whether to play or not to play, and how to govern your choices.

Starting from the recognition that personal power is the foundation for all other kinds, I make the point that personal power is derived from your style and tactics, and suggest practical guidelines for you to develop your own style and tailor your tactics to suit your ethics and energy. I explain why the main fuels of personal power are patience and drive and include suggestions to help you find and develop your own versions of patience and drive. A process for de-dramatizing your crises and de-escalating your stress is also included.

A *Force of Ones* closes with a final look at the principles of individualism and its fundamentals, and why becoming an individual is worth the effort.

CHAPTER TWELVE

Power and Politics: To Play or Not to Play

THIS CHAPTER is about power and politics and your relationship to them. It starts by sharpening the definitions of those terms and advising you to get comfortable with them. Then it asks you to ask yourself what you want in the way of power (kind and amount) and what you're willing to invest (energy and concentration) to get it. It also asks to what extent you want to be a power player.

If you evolve a realistic balance between the two sides of the power equation—the output you want and the energy you're willing and able to put in—you are less likely to disappoint yourself. For instance, if you're only willing to work forty-five hours a week and you strongly disapprove of politics, you probably won't get to be a CEO.

This chapter also looks at style, technique, and personal characteristics as components of power and politics. You'll learn to recognize these factors in your environment, and I'll suggest that you pick one or two techniques to try out for yourself. The chapter closes with a set of political guidelines for implementing a major project.

The politics and power I discuss here are not the hardball

kind. Those are beyond both the scope of this book and the expertise of its writer. I have certainly known hardball players— for example, one executive who used private detectives to gather background information on competitors, and one who sponsored an illegal break-in (like guess who), also to get information. I could understand how being involved in that sort of activity might be exciting, but it was too spicy for my diet.

Getting Comfortable with Power and Politics

To some people, *politics* and *power* are dirty words. They've become synonymous with corruption and oppression, and they represent what's wrong with government and large organizations. Getting stuck in that orientation is a mistake. Not that corruption and oppression don't exist; they do, and there's lots of both around, but they don't define the concepts. According to *Webster's Ninth New Collegiate Dictionary*, power is "ability to act or produce an effect," and politics is "the art or science... [of] influencing...policy." Professional politicians perceive power to be indispensable to the continuation of civilization, and call politics "the art of the possible."

A point of view I like is that politics is how people influence each other in the process of getting things done in organizations. And power is about the patterns of competition and cooperation among individuals and interest groups as they pursue resources, authority, leadership, and other organizational advantages. Power and politics may be ethical or corrupt, oppressive or liberating. It all depends on the characters of the people involved.

Everyone who works in an organization becomes involved in

214

politics and power to some extent. It's unavoidable when people who have points of view, purposes, and egos deal with people who have other points of view, purposes, and egos. You may think of the processes involved as improper and intolerable. A friend of mine quit a job at a major Hollywood studio that paid very well and promised a great future because he felt more energy was being spent on politics than on making movies. You may think of politics and power as necessary evils that you have to overcome on the way to doing your job. Or you may think of politics and power as exciting sports—the best part of your job.

Those who hold the latter view we have come to identify as *players*. Serious players are in organizational politics for the long term. They were born with (or have acquired) a conviction that, as in other sports (as well as in all life's contests), there are cycles in organizational politics—ups and downs and momentum shifts—and they're willing and able to take them in stride.

Whether or not you love organizational politics or think of yourself as a player, if you are seriously interested in accomplishing your goals and translating your ideas into events, understanding some of the basics of power and politics is useful. If, like my friend, you find the amount and kind of power and politics in your organization intolerable, then, of course, you ought to leave.

Personal Power

In actuality, there are many kinds of power, and people who have one kind often lack another. For instance, I know a woman who runs a good size company and runs it crisply. She has, however, no power and little influence with her two teenage children.

There are basically two broad categories of power: personal and positional. Your positional power derives from the place you occupy in the hierarchy. Generally speaking, if you are the boss you have more power than your subordinate. Your personal power derives from the characteristics and skills you display and exercise as an individual. You've probably heard it said more than once that personal power is a state of mind. Confidence is a big component of personal power. Andrei Olhovskiy, a tennis player ranked 193 in the world, beat Jim Courier, the number one ranked player, at Wimbledon in 1992. Afterward Olhovskiy said, "Number one or number two hundred, it's all in the mind."

Generally speaking, confident people start with more potential power than those who are unsure and less adept. But that's not always the case; sometimes insecure people find other ways to get and hold power. They may work harder or smarter or more manipulatively. I believe that in the process of developing his or her individualism, each person must reestablish his or her personal core of confidence. The early part of this book, covering grounding, self-boundaries, and the I-senses, deals with ways to help you reestablish that core. Confidence, though, is only a starting point. You also need a clearer notion of your relationship to power and what you want from it.

Do you want more power? If so, you need to think about what kind, how much, and for what purpose. Look at the following short list. Say you have one hundred ergs of power to spend. How much would you invest in each of the following?

1. Making more dollars
2. Gaining higher position, status, and recognition
3. Making important decisions

4. Controlling others' actions
5. Exercising important influence
6. Maintaining your present place in the hierarchy
7. Winning the game
8. Being well thought of by your peers
9. Achieving important goals
10. Doing good and honorable things for others

To the extent that your investments are concentrated in items 3, 4, 5, and 7, you are probably a bona fide power player. You are looking for command and advantage. If you invested mostly in the other items, you may be more interested in being successful or accomplishing particular goals.

Political Basics: Style and Tactics

In every organization of any size anywhere in the world, and probably some on other worlds as well, there are people who know and practice the political techniques discussed next. There are two reasons for knowing something about these techniques. First, you'll be more likely to recognize them, and second, you can pick one or more to try out. My suggestion is to pick the ones that might be fun to work with, and skip the ones that make you uncomfortable. Some are relatively easy, requiring only a bit more awareness; others will require sustained concentration until they feel natural. If they never feel natural, forget them. Don't forget, successful people come in a large variety.

My bias in favor of straightforwardness will be evident in the techniques I have chosen to discuss. That bias has precluded coverage of a good many political techniques that involve circuitous or devious approaches. Again, before you take on any of the proposals below, check to see if it's right for you. Ask yourself if it fits with both your ideal values (what you believe in) and your operational values (what you actually tend to do). To understand the difference between these values, consider the CEO who had an intention to establish profit-sharing and stock option plans that would include the rank and file of the company. He carried that intention with him into three different companies he headed over two decades, but somehow, it never came to pass. He was a good CEO as well as a decent human being, but his operational values never caught up with his ideal values.

To check the rightness of a suggestion, also ask yourself:

- Does it feel okay—not unnatural?

- Can I do this in a way that's fun rather than a continual chore?

- Do I have the energy and commitment to sustain my effort?

Style

Style is symbolic. Your style—how you appear and how you behave—can be a badge of what you represent *and* the expression of your differentness. Frank Jascinski, an industrial psychologist, told the story of a manufacturing plant where assembly-line workers typically wore blue shirts and foremen wore white ones. But one assembly-line worker kept showing up in a white shirt. He was soon promoted to foreman. Jascinski's research indicated that it was primarily because management was so bothered by the discrepancy they had to "correct" it.

Be aware of the symbols you present in how you dress, what you drive, and so on. Of course, those things are superficial, but in many organizations, they are part of the political game. You can choose to go along with the prevailing mode or vary from it drastically. You can also put your own personal twist on your choice. For example, even if you're basically conservative and modest, pick a particular article of apparel and make it your personal symbol (for example, long collars or dark suits or green ties). Being aware of prevailing style doesn't mean slavishly following it. Bryan Burrough and John Helyar, in *Barbarians at the Gate: The Fall of RJR Nabisco* (1990), describe how, as a free-wheeling CEO at RJR Nabisco, Ross Johnson wore his hair long and often dressed informally but was also known to be super-latively sensitive to the power structures he worked with and to the rituals of the boardroom.

You don't need to take the exercise terribly seriously, just think of it as an opportunity to play dress-up. What's important about style is to select and develop one that fits you, and with which you can have a good time.

There are two aspects of personal style that are not always obvious but, I believe, are particularly worth considering as you make your choices. They come under the headings of *entertainment* and *generosity*.

Entertainment. If someone were to ask me to list important skills leaders ought to have, my list would include the ability to entertain. I'm not talking about social entertaining, but about at-work entertaining. A considerable part of the time people spend at work is spent under pressure or tension. To the extent you can divert, enliven, charm, or fascinate bosses, peers, and subordinates, you can get their attention and a favorable reception (at least to start) for your proposals. Whether it's a *good* joke at the beginning of a presentation, a novel interpretation, or a sharp aphorism that catches a complex concept in a few words, some time spent entertaining your audience can help.

You don't have to be a stand-up comedian to think of ways to introduce an element of fun from time to time into serious work. A manager I worked with during a very difficult project had a large paper banner printed which he hung in the central hallway of his building. It said, "This is March 23rd, the official low-point of this project." Other project personnel quickly added their own graffiti, including, "No wonder I feel so bad," and "There's nowhere to go from here but up."

Generosity. Each of us is generous sometimes and to some extent. My second recommendation about personal style is that, within the bounds of your own judgments, you favor your generous impulses. Being generous is usually a sound long-term strategy. If you're a boss considering matters of pay, perquisites, and privileges for your subordinates, a reasonably liberal interpretation is better than a parsimonious one.

Sharing the limelight for outstanding achievements with subordinates or co-workers is another aspect of generosity. Make the acknowledgment genuine and accurate, rather than Academy Award hyperbole. Finding a consolation prize for those to whom you have to say no can be especially useful. If you have to turn down a proposal made by a valued employee, see if there's a way to put her on the team for the proposal you did accept. Be polite and considerate to old codgers. And don't insult anyone you don't need to.

Finally, there's one kind of generosity that runs deeper than specific acts of largess. Genuine generosity is offered freely and without expectation of a return payoff. That's generosity of the spirit, and it cannot be compelled before its time. As a good friend of mine once said, "You get naturally generous when your own ticket has been punched often enough that you don't need to prove how good you are anymore. Then you can concentrate on other people."

Tactics

My intention here is to identify basic political tactics and to describe them in basic ways. Just about everything you read here will be familiar, "something," as Groucho used to say (and Cosby said later), "you see around the house every day."

• *Legitimate favors.* Exchanging favors with others has been a fundamental of political interaction since human organization began (and before that among primates). Doing a favor can be as easy as making an extra copy of your staff meeting notes for one of your peers who missed the meeting, or introducing people with potential mutual interests. It can be as complicated as changing one of your department's processes in order to facilitate the work of another department. One thing to remember about favors is don't be bashful about expecting reciprocation later, but don't turn bitter if you don't get it. (Remember, you're in this sport for the long haul.)

• *Trades and trade-offs.* If you want to become a better politician become a discoverer and inventor of trades and trade-offs. Concentrate on finding or developing a present or future advantage for the party with whom you're negotiating. Make it clear that if your peer cooperates with you on your project you'll give her credit when you present it to the boss. To expand your range of possibilities, think flexibly. Look beyond each situation to its surrounding circumstances for the possibility of side deals. For instance, if you need a report from another department tomorrow and they say they can't do it until next week, offer to loan them a clerk from your department to help, and maybe special consideration next time they want something from your department.

When you seem to be at an impasse, try to think of new ways to consider the issue. For example, a manager was continually disappointed by the failure of an otherwise excellent employee to submit regular status reports on major projects. The subordinate (who didn't think the status reports were important) grudgingly promised to do better in the future but never did. The mutual resentment they felt interfered with the rest of their work. In a counseling session, the manager was asked to state, in specific terms, what he wanted to get from the status reports. He identified a relatively few key dates and budget conformance data. After that, the two were readily able to agree on a much more concise format for the status report and a specified time block each month in which the subordinate would prepare it.

• *Skip-level relationships.* Meeting, making impressions on, and nurturing relationships with people at higher levels (including your boss's boss) is good politics. At the same time, be aware of your boss's sensitivities and avoid threatening them. It's not a bad idea to show off a little in front of high-level managers, as long as you're relevant and do not overdo it. Senior managers frequently pride themselves (or pretend to) on knowing the strengths and weaknesses of personnel at all levels of their organization. Yet in reality, they do not get a great deal of information on which to base their assessments. If you register a positive impression in only a meeting or two, that may be enough to notch you a place in an executive's memory and start building your reputation. If you want senior managers to pay attention to you, use your awareness and observation skills to learn their preferred styles and special interests (see Chapters Two and Seven). After a meeting, spend a few minutes making notes about what you observed. For example, what kinds of information or data seem to be most persuasive to the executive(s)? What variety of politics seems to be going on? The same general approach can apply to building positive contacts with others who are important to you, for example, the thought-leaders of groups with which you deal.

• *A modicum of shmoozing.* To shmooz, as Leo Rosten says in *The Joys of Yiddish*, is to have a "friendly . . . heart-to-heart talk," or "chat." Being an individual with opinions of your own does not require you to reject or ignore others' opinions. Good politics includes keeping up to date on prevailing opinion about the subjects that are important to you. If you are an operating manager, make friends with staffers rather than scorn them. Most of them will appreciate it. One division manager made it a point each time he went to New York to stop in and visit with corporate staff people (whom most of his peers studiously avoided). He asked their opinions and asked them to do a variety of studies for him. They turned out to be invaluable sources of information, both formal and informal, for him.

If you decide to pursue a direction that is counter to prevailing practice or opinion, start by identifying who might go along with you, who might be against you, and most important, who might go either way. Don't waste much time selling to those who are already sold or those who are clearly against. Spend your time with the undecided in what politicians call "the corridors of indifference." Feel the neutrals out and figure out what it would take to get them on the side of your proposal.

Finally, an old and frequently neglected fundamental: in most organizations, as trite as it may seem, nothing succeeds better than good work. Your reputation and credibility will be maintained and grown or undermined and shrunk based on your performance. Doing what you say you will do is key.

Notes:
Power and Politics

- Power is ability to produce an effect. Politics is the art of influencing policy. Neither is a dirty word. Both are parts of organizational sports, which some people love and others dislike. Whether you like power and politics or not, you ought to learn something about them.

- The particular political tactics you choose ought to fit your ethics and be fun (rather than burdensome) to exercise. If they aren't, you probably won't be able to sustain the energy you need to make them work.

- Style counts. If you have (or can develop) the ability to entertain, to socialize deftly, and to behave generously, you will have an advantage in most organizations. If your personal character is resistant to one or all of those behaviors, don't force yourself. There are other ways to spend your energy that also pay off.

- Exchanging favors and negotiating trades are the key tactics of politics. Use your expanded awareness to discover opportunities for your own and others' present or future advantage.

-

CHAPTER THIRTEEN

Patience and Drive:
The Yin and Yang of Character

THE FIRST PART of this chapter is about intangibles, the underlying traits of temperament. The traits are patience and drive—sort of the yin and yang of character. The last part of the chapter deals with the stresses that almost invariably go along with life in organizations, and I outline an unconventional but often effective process for converting stress into more useful energy.

The World Gets Fair—Eventually

Max Kohlberg was manager of Product Engineering in Jane Romano's Product Design division. He was bright, knew his business, and paid attention to detail. In February, his department completed an important study on the producibility of a new component. To assure the accuracy and quality of the study report, Max and his secretary worked one evening until midnight preparing and proofing the next-to-final drafts. On the day for preparing and submitting the final report, however, Max's secretary became seriously ill with the flu and wasn't able to complete the final draft of the report. Before going home, she

227

arranged for a typist from the typing pool to finish the work. The morning of that same day, Max himself was called at home by Jane Romano and asked to fly to Cleveland right away to handle an emergency assignment.

The typist sent over from the typing pool that afternoon was a temporary employee, hired for the week because the flu epidemic had caused a high absence rate in the pool. She was a poor typist and careless, and she made many mistakes in the report. Later that same afternoon, Jane called Max's department, and one of the young engineers who was in Max's outer office at the time took the call. Jane asked, in what to the young engineer seemed an impatient tone, whether the report was finished. In a near panic to respond to the big boss, the young engineer took it upon himself to hover around the temporary typist as she typed the report, thereby increasing both her nervousness and her errors. When she finally typed the last page he quickly clipped the pages together and hand-delivered them to Jane.

When Max returned to his office two days later, weary from his long hours of work with the Cleveland emergency, he was immediately called to Jane's office and criticized severely for the many errors in the report. Max said nothing.

In a mid March staff meeting, a problem was raised about a cost overrun on one of the division's product development projects. Attention was focused on the design engineering manager; however, without quite saying so, the design engineering manager hinted broadly that part of the fault was attributable to Max's department. In fact, this was not so. Max, however, said nothing.

In April, Max was again called to Jane Romano's office. She

greeted him warmly, shook his hand, and congratulated him on the development of a lower-cost method for testing components. One entire process had been eliminated in the test sequence without affecting reliability. Jane told Max the accomplishment wouldn't be forgotten at bonus time. It was only after listening for a while that Max remembered that the elimination had been accidental, based on his own oversight. He said nothing.

The Intangibles of Operating Style: Patience

Patience is the ability to wait. It includes the capacity to endure ambiguous and difficult times with composure and to function well in times of suspense when you don't know how issues you feel strongly about will turn out, or even in adversity when issues turn out badly. The higher you move in organizational hierarchies, the more you deal with longer-term issues, the more important patience gets. Max's story illustrates one aspect of patience. There are others. Patience is a requirement in just about all organizational sports.

In my work as a management consultant, I've worked with and followed the careers of a number of people over ten and sometimes twenty years. The one thing almost all have had in common is serious ups and downs in their careers. For instance, one climbed the ladder from junior engineer to division manager in record time for his company. Then, because his arrogance became intolerable to too many people, he was demoted to department manager.

Two years later, because he was so bright and seemed to have learned a bit of humility, he was repromoted to head another

229

division. Over the next ten years, he was promoted several more times until he became a senior officer of the company, its most successful operating manager, and according to many, most likely to become the company's next CEO. Three years later, by mutual agreement, he left the company. The operating revenues of his business units were below expectations. A year and a half later, he joined with a group of investors to form and head a new company. And the story continues.

One important thing to remember is that organizational games seldom end (except *perhaps* at retirement), so victories are almost never permanent nor are defeats. As long as you keep playing, the game just keeps going and going.

Patience can help you to pace yourself and your tactics over both the short and the long term. You can think of this as operational patience. A basic example of operational patience is not shooting all your bullets in your first proposal. It may be better to provide your audience with what you think they can absorb in one sitting and save some ammunition for the next session. Plan campaigns rather than battles.

An ancient truism holds that timing is everything. Approaching those you are trying to influence at the right time is critical. Usually that means when the subject is an important concern but not a crisis. If your proposal has to do with changing the company's shipping procedures, you probably don't want to make it while everyone is frantically running around trying to clear mountains of merchandise off the docks, but a day or two afterward might be just right.

When you make presentations aimed at marketing your proposal, focus on what's important to your boss and other decision makers rather than what most interests you. Take the time to anticipate and prepare answers for the hard questions bosses love to ask: What for? How much? How long? How sure?

A reputation for patience, persistence, and endurance will help you mobilize effort from others. They have to know you're serious and your proposals aren't just passing whims that will be blown away by the first squall of opposition. And when your proposal prevails in the battle for acceptance, that doesn't mean the war is won. Be ready to endure early missteps and setbacks as you climb the learning curve to making your idea work.

Finally, for the person who truly believes in his or her idea, there is this to keep in mind. At times, whether your political skills are good or bad, the answer from above to your proposal will not turn out the way you want. So, if your bosses won't do things the way you think they ought to be done, then do those things the way they can be done and wait. Your turn will come again if you keep yourself in the lineup.

The Intangibles of Operating Style: Drive

Drive is probably *the* crucial dimension of power. A person with extraordinary drive directed toward a particular goal can often make things happen (whether he or she consciously follows the suggestions in this chapter or not). Drive is an intangible that's made up of fascination, inclination, and physical and mental energy. People with extraordinary drive are noticeable. They don't give up; they persist, not always pleasantly.

Those of us who have a less intense degree of drive in our makeups need to use what we have selectively. One way to be selective is to use a self-calibrating process. Deliberately ask yourself how much energy you really have and want to make

231

available for a particular goal or plan. A realistic equation that balances what you want with what you're willing to invest can prevent useless frustration and self-criticism.

The drive-evaluation exercise can help you to clarify your goal and identify the drive you have available for it. See if answering the questions in the exercise changes your energy level. If it doesn't, I suggest that you reexamine your goal. Maybe there is something you want more than your original goal. If you identify another goal, try the same list of questions on it.

Exercise: Drive Evaluation

Identify your situation or goal concisely in writing, then write your answers to these seven questions, or say them out loud. If you like, use the dialogue technique described in Chapter Five.

1. Do I really want to do anything about this situation other than I am already doing?

2. What do I want and what's the advantage of having it?

3. What do I want to avoid?

4. What will it take from me to reach my goal?

5. What's in the way?

6. What's likely to happen if I do nothing?

7. Is the answer to question six really a major problem?

De-dramatization

Selig was a young manager of labor relations for his company. After prodigious negotiations, he and the union representative he dealt with, an oldster who had been around since the first dawn, seemed to have arrived at an agreement on a particular work practice issue, though the agreement wasn't put in writing. Everything went well for almost two months, and then, abruptly, the union agent submitted a grievance on that practice. This seemed to Selig to violate their agreement. Disappointed and baffled by the action, he called a meeting with the old union rep where he recounted in inexhaustible detail his recollection of their previous conversation. The union rep merely sat impassively and listened without response. Selig's frustration grew until he finally threw up his hands and said dramatically, "I don't understand how we can continue to work together if we can't depend on each other's word."

The union rep sat for a moment, head bent, looking up at Selig through grizzled gray eyebrows. "Selig," he said, "as bad as it gets now and then, just keep in mind, if it wasn't for guys like me, there wouldn't be any need to hire guys like you." Then he grinned fondly at the young union relations manager.

Let's be clear about this. As though plain old ordinary survival wasn't tough enough in organizations these days, the power and politics aspects of survival make the situation even more complicated and stressful. For a lot of people, especially those who don't like the emotional tensions and anxieties that full involvement in the political arena seems to engender in them, it's a lot simpler, and easier on the stomach, just to do the job the way they think they ought to and not worry about all the stuff they find distasteful. Maybe politics is going on all around you, but that doesn't mean you have to get involved in it, does it?

Up to a certain point, probably not. If you are reasonably good at your specialty, you can probably afford to ignore politics until your talents carry you to the upper-middle-management level. After that, if you don't at least learn to recognize what's going on, you are probably going to find yourself frustrated as your good ideas and intentions keep crashing against political rocks you never even noticed. As one CEO said to me, "When you get beyond middle management, intelligence isn't what it's about. It's a new game. In a good organization, just about everyone near the top is smart enough, but smart isn't what counts most."

If you are an individual who is often more dismayed and vexed than positively stimulated by the tensions you encounter from your organization's political dramas, here's a suggestion for coping with the stresses. Learn to *de-dramatize* the situations you confront and to deal with them at several phenomenological levels rather than just one.

For instance, let's say that you made an agreement with a co-worker. Your plans depended on her keeping the agreement, but she didn't. And this is not the first time that's happened to you in working with her. Getting mad or fantasizing a way to get even may be your first reaction when you feel you have been crossed by someone else, but it's seldom useful (or healthful) to hold grudges. You might as well hold a grudge against the desert for being too hot and dry.

When you're upset, anxious, angry, or otherwise overly emotional about a person or situation, your mind is less likely to have access to a full range of options. Converting your bottled-up feelings to a more constructive form often yields both a reduction in stress and better ideas for action.

An exercise that takes people through the dynamics of a situation has helped many people I've worked with to discharge dysfunctional stress and see available actions more clearly. It's based on a set of straightforward assumptions and a somewhat unconventional way of putting them to use. The assumptions are these. Each stress-producing *situation*, for example, the unmet expectation a person has of a co-worker, evokes an *emotion* such as anger in the victim-participant. Further, that emotion produces (or at least coincides with) a *physical tension* within the body. (For example, the victim-participant tightens his or her shoulder muscles.)

That physical tension contains within itself the optimum blueprint for its most appropriate *kinesthetic release*, or movement toward relaxation (perhaps a slow, forward roll of the shoulders or stretching the chest muscles). And finally, this kinesthetic release is often accompanied by corresponding changes in the way the victim-participant feels the emotional and perceives the situational aspects of the experience. Because all these phenomena—situation, emotion, tension, release—are linked in a chain, when you allow the last link in the chain to complete itself and change, you favorably affect all the prior links. The process is fairly simple, and it's not necessary for you to "believe" in it for it to work. Just try the exercise the next time you find yourself irritated, agitated, or stewing about a situational drama and see what happens.

Exercise:
From Situation to Dynamic and Back

1. *Situation.* In a quiet place where you won't be disturbed, find a comfortable, but not overly upholstered chair. Close your eyes and picture yourself involved with the problem and the person or persons whom you see as the cause of the problem. To the extent you are able, visualize the scene.

2. *Emotion.* Identify in your mind the particular emotion this situation evokes in you—sadness, discouragement, anxiety, anger, and so forth. Forget about the situation and concentrate on the emotion. *Where* in your body is that emotion?

3. *Physical tension.* Shift your attention to your body, exploring from feet to head, inside and out, the particular stress, strain, or pressure that connects to that emotion. Don't worry about being absolutely sure about the connection. Focus on the body signal that seems most compelling. Forget about the emotion the signal represents and concentrate on the physical feeling.

4. *Kinesthetic release.* Center your awareness on the tension to see what it "wants" to do—how its energy tends to push or

236

pull your body. Does it want to stretch? To contract? To carry your whole body forward? Let go of any inclination you may have to interpret or judge the motion. Instead, merely allow your body to move as the tension seems to dictate. Continue until the process is done (for now). You'll know when that happens.

5. *Situation.* Relax in your chair again and gently return your imagination to the situation you began with in step 1. Check your thoughts and feelings for changes and see if you have some new ideas about dealing with the situation.

1

It's not difficult to be powerful
Nor to be powerless.
Each of us makes the choice,
Some for one
Some for the other.

The advantages and disadvantages
Of being powerful are
That you may think well of yourself
Or badly
As you choose,
That you may take action
Or stop the action of others
For a while.
You may assume responsibility
Or make others responsible
And hold them to account.

If you choose to be powerful
Others may look to you for guidance
Or pretend to.

They may honor you
Or hate you,
Rally to your cause
Or abandon you,
And that may be
Because of what you do
Or the way they are.

2

The advantages and disadvantages
Of being powerless are
That you may think well of yourself
Or badly
As you choose,
That you need not act
But may be acted upon,
That someone else, not you,
May carry your head and heart
From place to place,
Your burden thus reduced.

If you are powerless
You may disclaim responsibility
And complain and obstruct.

If you are powerless
Others may give you their sympathy
Or pretend to.

If you choose to be powerless
The weight upon your shoulders
May be heavy
If you tell yourself you are oppressed
And do nothing to change it
Or considerably lighter
If you confess to yourself
That other matters are
More compelling to you than power
Or if you choose
To shrug your shoulders and decide
To become powerful too.

But this relief, of course,
Is only temporary.
For then you will begin
Almost at once
To assume the burdens
Of the powerful.

Notes:
Patience and Drive

- The world gets fair—eventually.

- Patience and drive are the key traits of politically effective people. Patience is the capacity to wait in spite of the temptation to plunge ahead. Drive is the capacity to move ahead in spite of the temptation to quit.

- De-dramatization is a means to convert stress to positive action.

-

CHAPTER FOURTEEN

The Spirit of Individualism: Amazing Grace

CARL ROGERS, Abraham Maslow, and Frederick Perls were among the seminal contributors to the contemporary psychology of people in organizations. The works of all three were predicated on the uniqueness of the individual human being. They saw each of us as a free agent with an inborn tendency to realize his or her own potential. Maslow, in particular, in his 1982 book *Toward a Psychology of Being*, presented a model for the development of the person that included the "peak experience," a person's individual encounter with the best within himself or herself—an opportunity for the person to surpass his or her ordinary level of functioning or perception and reach a new summit of performance or insight.

In an important sense, *A Force of Ones* is about new summits of performance in leadership, whether it's the leadership of managers who run organizations or the leadership of single contributors who only run themselves. Basically, *individualism is leadership*, and leadership requires a willingness to depart from time to time from what is popular and conventional. Leadership also requires that you know what you want, what most needs doing, and which paths are the most likely ones to get you what you want.

Individualism is important to each of us. That it continues to exist and flourish is also important to our society. Just as high-quality products can only be made of high-quality parts, better communities, better teams, and better coalitions can be built only if they are built of confident, competent, and congruent individuals. Accumulations of the dependent, anxious, and discouraged will be more likely to produce narrow protectiveness than improvement.

The Ascent of Demographics and Decline of Individualism

In large organizations, interest in individuals declined significantly in the big systems–oriented 1980s. Even now, we live in an age captivated by measures of central tendencies among large populations and are made impatient and confused by the variations of individual cases. We are infatuated by demographics, the statistical study of human distributions. Even the relatively few individual-employee development approaches that survive in organizations are "validated" and interpreted according to statistical distributions derived from mass testing. You answer a series of questions, total your score, and check with the table provided in order to find how you compare to large numbers of people who supposedly hold similar jobs in other companies. We seem to be much more devoted to slotting our characteristics into pigeonholes than to experiencing and contributing the varied and unique aspects of ourselves.

Is It Hard to Be an Individual?

Writers and psychologists do not see individualism as easy. Some see it as challenging, others as terrifying. Writing in the first half of the century, Swiss psychologist Carl Jung recognized the importance of individualism in human development, but he also acknowledged the pains of becoming an individual, writing, "The process of individuation does not come easily to a man or woman and with most people it does not proceed very far. Most men go to their graves as children. They embrace a 'participation mystique' with the life of the group to replace the parents. This allows them to run their customary repetitive pathways unconscious, as an animal moves from game to water. Becoming an individual occurs only rarely, and then only through dislodgement by the severest shocks."

Psychoanalyst Helmuth Kaiser wrote that individualism "is our Achilles heel. We can not stand to be a single person. We are marching along, keeping in line. There is order and symmetry as we go. It is as if one mind controls each movement and each thought of all. It is only when we encounter a rock and must decide individually whether to pass on the right or the left that the horrible truth of our individuality becomes undeniable."

I have saved for several years a comment made by a writer whose name is unknown to me. He or she spoke of "the third of the Chinese Facts of Life—the intense wish to bathe in the warm soup of cultural identity, to proclaim self as part of a 'we' and have others affirm, absolutely. The life into which we are born is, ordinarily, life within family. The family is the first 'we.' Usually, in the course of a lifetime, one 'we' leads to and coalesces with the next. The pain associated with dissolution of 'we' or the discovery that there was no 'we' in the first place is one of the greatest shocks in life."

And finally, of course, there is Henry David Thoreau's famous observation in *Walden*, back in 1854, "If a man does not keep pace with his companions, perhaps it is because he hears a different drummer. Let him step to the music which he hears, however measured or far away."

Frankly, while I appreciate the dramatic power of the preceding comments, I do not think the prospects for individuation are nearly so daunting. Maybe it's a matter of the differences between the present and the earlier parts of our century when those I quoted mostly spoke and wrote. Perhaps our culture has been so pummeled by the pace of radical and seemingly irresistible changes brought by technology and science that it can't mobilize itself as well for resistance to individualism, nor for sustaining the kinds of support and reward it once promised for conformity.

The Spirit of Individualism

Individualism is discovering your own singular vision and bringing it to life. It's tapping into your own unique energy and determination and using them to build your personal power. It's using that power, sometimes in combination with others and sometimes alone, to make ordinary and occasionally extraordinary things happen. While individualism is perhaps not as difficult as it once was, it is not easy either, nor is it for everyone. In fact, people who choose individualism often do so because circumstances and their own characters propel them to it. Is individualism for you? It is if you have

- A need to know who's there under your suit of clothes
- An enthusiasm for deciding your own decisions and choosing your own choices
- A readiness to go your own way, at your own speed
- An inclination to explore outside the lines, and to risk diverging from the norms of your peers
- A willingness to change your mind

Getting into Individualism

Even if you have the inclination toward individualism, you will still have to step off some of your oldest and most comfortable treadmills, those that are firmly and unquestioningly supported by your business and social peer groups. Such treadmills as the sanctity of quarterly results, measuring your significance according to the level of your pay and perks, and gauging your life according to the size of your house, what you drive, and all those other old familiar signposts.

Chances are that most people won't step off any treadmill as long as it's carrying their weight tolerably well. Individualism is most likely to rear its head in times of crisis, when an old, dependable structure of job or family somehow tumbles down. You suddenly realize you are in the middle of the resulting heap, and you know that you have to be the person in charge of managing yourself out of it. No matter how much or little sympathy and support you get from others, you are going to have to use your own resources and make your own choices.

When I spoke with the CEO of a very large company who was about to retire and was going through intense separation pains, he wondered what he would do afterward, and was even more worried about "doing nothing." He vividly recalled his bypass surgery and reflected on his own mortality. He was, in his words, "worrying about those same old gremlins," some of which had been around for years and years. The CEO was a person about to be dislodged. What were his options? To struggle to hold on to what he had, or as close to it as he could manage? Or to look and see something new for which to strive? Or not to strive at all? There's certainly no single answer that's best for everybody. What's important for the CEO (and for each of us) is that the options can be seen clearly, and truly considered with both the mind and the I-senses.

Relative Realities

Norms, values, and even realities in present-day society have become exceedingly insubstantial. Television reflects the radically changing norms of sex, family, morality, and ethics. Of course, talk about reestablishing traditional values, especially traditional "family values," continues, but how practicable is that when close to half our families are configurations of single parents, single parents living with an other-than-married partner, and so on? If traditional values are dissolving, can anyone make them firm again?

Mark Backman, a contemporary writer and teacher, says in an unpublished work (1992) that truth is relative for most people and that we operate together on the basis of "contingent verisimilitudes—temporary operational realities based on what we can agree upon at any given moment."

248

As if to confirm and epitomize his view, one of the newest stars in the firmament of political specialists nowadays is the *spin doctor*. The spin doctor's job is to look at situations, especially negative ones, involving a political candidate/patient and reinterpret (spin) those situations so that they can be presented in a positive light. High unemployment statistics are compared against past statistics that were even higher, or they are acknowledged but blamed on another branch of government. An action portrayed as seriously harmful to the environment by one side's spin doctors is portrayed as a major contribution to job formation by the other's.

Thus we live in a time of flimsy values and relative realities. Flux, turbulence, quick change, and insecurity surround us, and when we try to recapture such old stabilities as family values, they no longer seem to fit our requirements. Worse yet, when we abandon norms and values while still pretending to ourselves that we hold them, we run into the problems and punishments of hypocrisy. When we introject the spins of social code words and such arbiters as political correctness as though they were real meanings, we restrict our possibilities severely. As long as we focus our arguments and attention on whether or not inner-city violence is a result of racism, we won't address what it's about and what can be done about it from an operational standpoint. To the extent that we fixate on a "war on drugs" and "just say no" slogans, we won't examine possibilities that fall beyond those frameworks.

The Restless Dead

When we pretend to ourselves that we believe the positions we espouse, our doubts are not quenched, and no number of antacid tablets will stop the burning. Skepticism and cynicism spread through our belief systems until everything is regarded with unadmitted but unstoppable doubt.

You and I are our own spin doctors. When our dialogues with ourselves and others are limited to exchanging slogans, party lines, and wishful thinking, they can lead us only to old conclusions. Difficult, uncomfortable issues can be obscured, evaded, even buried, but they are likely to be restless dead.

Individualism is the tendency to confront difficult dilemmas rather than evade them. There are times for hitching up your jeans and looking the predicament in the eye. When you're scared, that's part of the equation, but it doesn't have to be a showstopper.

Inventing Your Own Exercises

The earlier chapters of this book contained exercises for use in particular circumstances. If you've read them carefully, and especially if you've tried a few, you probably have noticed the pattern that underlies most of them. It is

- Calm down
- Suspend judgment
- Survey your environment/situation
- Tap into your own wants and clarify them
- Mobilize your energy and resources in the way that best fits *you*
- Act, track, and adjust

Once you understand this pattern, you can use it to invent your own exercises, tailoring them to fit your self and your circumstances. But, as an individual, you must still remember that, when it comes right down to it, the pattern is no more than one more prescription, and it's only the right one when you're ready for it to be. Each of us has to do what each of us has to do. When each of us is done with that, he or she goes on to the next thing. Being ready for the next thing is a matter of grace.

Amazing Grace

I can't talk about the spirit of individualism without a word about grace—amazing grace. What is grace? Grace is fitness of line and shape and time. Grace is beauty in movement. Grace is feeling in harmony. Grace is finding and being in the zone, in your groove, in your best place. Grace is doing it *right*.

Your singular vision appears to you when grace grants it. You find the surge of courage and confidence to venture off the well-worn paths of convention, whether it's to consider a potential new product or market, start a new business, or take a year's sabbatical to sail around the world or work in the Peace Corps when grace says it's time.

You decide to be a singular person, to poke your head above the warm soup of your cultural identity, to discover you always were a singular person anyway, right on schedule. It's all in grace's hands.

Not hollow as an onion but as a bowl that contains it all.

You don't have to be a rocket scientist
Or a brain surgeon
Or an NFL quarterback
Or a Fortune-listed CEO
To take charge of what's most important,
You.

In fact, you can't avoid being in charge.
You may try to hand yourself off to others
But they'll eventually disappoint you.
They won't solve your problems
Or take responsibility for your mistakes—
They're too busy with their own.
No one can fix your life but you,
It's you or nobody.

If you want a change
There are others who can point out paths
But you have to travel them yourself
And carry your own lamp.
That way, the road is a good one
The discoveries are fascinating
And they're really yours.

Notes:
The Spirit of Individualism

References

Backman, M. *The Third Sophistic and the Search for Self*. Unpublished manuscript, 1992.

Burns, J. M. *Leadership*. New York: HarperCollins, 1978.

Burrough, B., and Helyar, J. *Barbarians at the Gate: The Fall of RJR Nabisco*. New York: HarperCollins, 1990.

Dos Passos, J. *One Man's Initiation*. London: Allen & Unwin, 1920.

Drucker, P. Seminar presentation, 1970.

Fagan, J., and Shepherd, I. L. *Gestalt Therapy Now*. Mountain View, Calif.: Science and Behavior Books, 1970.

Maslow, A. *Toward a Psychology of Being* (2nd ed.). New York: Van Nostrand Reinhold, 1982.

Norton, N. *The Digital Equipment Corporation Networking Case Study*. Nolan-Norton Institute, 1988.

Perls, F. S. *Gestalt Therapy Verbatim*. Moab, Utah: Real People Press, 1969.

Rosten, L. *The Joys of Yiddish*. New York: Simon & Schuster, 1991.

Thoreau, H. D. *Walden*. New York: Vintage, 1991 [1854].

Webster's Ninth New Collegiate Dictionary. Springfield, Mass.: Merriam-Webster, 1985.

Index